Management and Industrial Relations Series

5

Power in a trade union

Management and Industrial Relations Series

Editors:

DOROTHY WEDDERBURN
Principal of Bedford College, London

MICHAEL BROMWICH
Professor of Finance and Accounting, University of Reading

and

DOUGLAS BROOKS
Director, Walker Brooks and Partners

Social science research has much to contribute to the better understanding and solution of problems in the field of management and industrial relations. The difficulty, however, is that there is frequently a gap between the researcher and the practitioner who wants to use the research results. This new series is designed to make available to practitioners in the relevant fields the results of the best research which the Economic and Social Research Council (ESRC) has supported in the fields of management and industrial relations. The subjects covered and the style adopted will appeal to managers, trade unionists and administrators because there will be an emphasis upon the practical implications of research findings. But the volumes will also serve as a useful introduction to particular areas for students and teachers of management and industrial relations.

The series is published by Cambridge University Press in collaboration with the Economic and Social Research Council.

Other books in the series

1 *Lost managers: supervisors in industry and society* by JOHN CHILD and BRUCE PARTRIDGE
2 *Tackling discrimination in the workplace: an analysis of sex discrimination in Britain* by BRIAN CHIPLIN and PETER SLOANE
3 *Inflation accounting: an introduction to the debate* by GEOFFREY WHITTINGTON
4 *Industrial relations and management strategy* edited by KEITH THURLEY and STEPHEN WOOD

Power in a trade union

The role of the district committee in the AUEW

by

LARRY JAMES

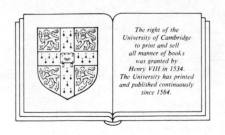

The right of the
University of Cambridge
to print and sell
all manner of books
was granted by
Henry VIII in 1534.
The University has printed
and published continuously
since 1584.

CAMBRIDGE UNIVERSITY PRESS

Cambridge
London   New York   New Rochelle
Melbourne   Sydney

Published by the Press Syndicate of the University of Cambridge
The Pitt Building, Trumpington Street, Cambridge CB2 1RP
32 East 57th Street, New York, NY 10022, USA
296 Beaconsfield Parade, Middle Park, Melbourne 3206, Australia

First published 1984

Printed in Great Britain at
the University Press, Cambridge

Library of Congress catalogue card number: 83-7673

British Library Cataloguing in Publication Data

James, Larry
Power in a trade union: the role of the district
committee in the AUEW.—(Management and industrial
relations; 5)
1. Amalgamated Union of Engineering Workers
I. Title II. Series
331.88′00941   TA157

ISBN 0 521 25798 0

SE

Contents

Preface

Most of the preparatory research on which this monograph is based was financed by the Social Science Research Council and made possible by the facilities of the University of Salford. Thanks are due to both these bodies for their support.

As the case studies concern actual events a great debt is owed to the participants for their willingness to help me reconstruct these events as accurately as possible. In particular, I should like to express my appreciation to Eddie Frow, former District Secretary to the Manchester district committee, for allowing me access to district records and the use of his own extensive library of labour history, for his help in gaining the co-operation of other participants, and for the unfailing patience he showed in the face of my sometimes naive questioning. The basis of the case studies is taken from the minutes of district committee and sub-committee meetings. It was Eddie Frow who first supervised their collation and binding as a permanent record of district committee work and I am pleased that the present District Secretary, Bill Mather, is continuing the practice.

The initial phase of the research consisted of analysing these minutes for the 1945 to 1970 period (1,250 sets of minutes in total). This analysis was then supplemented by other district records (letters and pamphlets, for example), by documents made available to me by the staff of the AUEW Research Department, and by lengthy interviews with key participants.

In the writing of the monograph I must acknowledge a debt to my academic colleagues for their advice, particularly to Professor Ray Loveridge of the University of Aston, who contributed greatly to the development of the ideas. I have to take full responsibility for the remaining limitations in methodology, conceptualisation and style of presentation.

L. E. J.
March 1982

vii

1
The democratic ideal

Introduction

Since the turn of the century when the Webbs published their *Industrial Democracy* and Michels his *Political Parties* there has been a reluctant consensus that in representative organisations like trade unions, democratic government, in which the rank and file have control over the important decisions, inevitably gives way to oligarchy, in which power is concentrated in the hands of a few chief officers and popular control becomes little more than a myth.

Trade unions in Britain are rarely short of critics and the apparent absence of democratic control has provided more ammunition with which they can be attacked. Yet the fundamental questions about the internal organisation of trade unions have been only partially resolved. How is it that organisations representing such a diversity of interests manage to hang together at all? How far do union members have to give up the right to dissent in order to achieve gains in the wider society? What is meant by popular control?

Michels (1958 edn) argued that the influence of committees, the formalities of bureaucracy, the stability of leadership and the greed for power would combine with the apathy of the masses to produce an inexorable tendency away from democracy towards oligarchy. His familiar proposition that 'who says organisation, says oligarchy' (1958: 401) has become the rallying standard for those who argue that oligarchy is inevitable and that the pursuit of democratic ideals is bound to fail.

Michels' analysis drew on the work of the Webbs who, though not as pessimistic, nevertheless felt that as unions grew they would leave behind the ideal of primitive democracy. Its place would be taken by what the Webbs regarded as the modern form of democracy, in which an elected representative assembly would appoint and control an executive committee to direct a permanent official staff (1920: 37). It is perhaps an irony that the Webbs' model of democracy, implying as it does high levels of participation at trade union branches, the election of officers and a key role for delegate conferences, should provide a basis for the argument that in practice trade unions are oligarchies. It has been observed and reobserved on numerous occasions that attendance at branch meetings is low. Goldthorpe *et al.* (1968) found that as many as 60 per cent of their sample of Vauxhall car workers had never attended a branch meeting, Brooks (1975) found that only 4 per cent of London busmen attended their branch, Fryer (in an internal study for the National Union of Public Employees in 1975) that 67 per cent of NUPE branches reported that no more than 5 per cent of members attended, and Moran (1974) that 60 per cent of uniformed staff of the Union of Post Office Workers never or only occasionally went to branch meetings. Similarly, the turnout for union elections is remarkably small (still less than 40 per cent in the AUEW even though postal balloting was introduced in 1972), and in many unions full-time officers are appointed rather than elected. Delegate conferences tend to be unwieldy events, the bulk of resolutions bearing little or no relation to the day-to-day issues of running the union. The size of such gatherings (the Union of Post Office Workers conference has over 1,000 delegates, for example) and the infrequency of the meetings make them unlikely mechanisms of popular control.

It has been suggested that faced with this inability to influence the decisions which affect their working lives trade union members can exercise the option of 'voting with their feet'. However, even before the spread of the closed shop, this argument was never very convincing. Both Clegg (1970) and Martin (1968) have noted that there is a low association between trends in union membership and other measures of dissatisfaction. Indeed, membership of the Union of Shop, Distributive and Allied Workers increased between 1949 and 1950 in spite of internal dissent leading to a defeat for executive policy at the 1950 annual conference. Similarly, the low success rate of breakaway unions suggests that they offer a poor remedy for groups of frustrated union members. The larger union almost invariably seeks the support of the employer in denying recognition to the breakaway group and, as Lerner's (1961) study of the Post Office Engineering Union showed, without recognition the break-away unions quickly disappear.

It may be asked whether it even matters that trade unions seem not to conform to the democratic ideal. As Allen (1954) pointed out, the unions exist to achieve certain economic ends, not to provide their members with an exercise in self-government. This is a persuasive line of reasoning, particularly when members themselves profess not to take an interest in the government of their union. Bealey has even posed the question 'How undemocratic is it to decide freely to be led by an oligarchy?' (1977: 394). There are a number of reasons why this argument misses the point. To begin with it assumes that members are not interested in *any* of the issues of union government, and that only economic ends are important. It is equally dangerous to assume that members are passive because they concur with the policies of the leadership. They may be unaware of these policies, or whether the policies are in their own interests. Alternatively, the members may be very aware of the policies and harbouring a sense of grievance which only requires an issue, or some organisation, to be brought to the surface in an explosive fashion. Hyman (1975: 83) has gone so far as to argue that passive democracy is not democracy at all.

The democratic ideal matters also because of the nature of the organisation. Hemingway quotes an affronted Bridgend busman: 'To use threats against its members! Had it been any other kind of organisation it wouldn't have been so bad' (1978: 110). There is an expectation that unions will be democratic, and if this expectation is not realised then members may be more difficult to control. It will be easier to enforce a decision which has been demonstrably arrived at democratically than one which has not.

It matters finally because trade union activity does not end at the place of work. The role of unions in the Labour Party and in the machinery of government ensures that unions have an important say on issues which affect more than their memberships. In order to exercise this role effectively trade union leaders need to be able to say with authority that they speak for their members. Where this is clearly not the case then credibility is lost and an important vehicle of social reform may be jeopardised.

Parties and factions

Although the formal constraints on oligarchy appear to be weak, and breaking away from the union is rarely an effective remedy, an important role in limiting the spread of oligarchic practices has been ascribed to the development of parties and factions within unions. Dissent may coalesce into opposition groups of varying degrees of permanence. In their classic work *Union Democracy* (1956) Lipset, Trow and Coleman identified within the International Typographical Union (ITU) the institutionalisation of opposition as the factor maintaining democracy. In the ITU this was provided by two recognised rival groups which competed openly at elections, the minority group having a reasonable chance of gaining a majority of offices and forming the administration. The authors remain pessimistic however, arguing that unless this two-party system is in operation a union is unlikely to be democratic. This definition is remarkably narrow and, as Clegg (1970) has suggested, if Lipset *et al.*'s categories are used the ITU becomes the deviant case of the only democratic trade union in the world.

Perhaps more important than the institutionalisation of opposition is the possibility that opposition can exist and flourish at all. Even so, organised opposition does not guarantee democracy. Martin (1968) suggests that democracy exists where there are limitations on a union executive's ability to prevent opposition factions forming, distributing propaganda and mobilising electoral support. The factions themselves are comparatively unstructured groups whose membership fluctuates according to the issues in dispute, and are significantly less permanent groupings than the parties identified by Lipset *et al.*

The factions model of government draws attention to the centrality of conflict to the decision-making process. Hemingway has developed this point to argue that since trade unions are pluralistic organisations conflict is inevitable. The process of government he describes is that of bargaining and negotiation between the various interests that make up the union. Occasionally this bargaining becomes acrimonious and the manifest conflict reveals the processes of control at work in the union.

It is equally true that factions may exist for years without success and make little contribution to democracy. Edelstein (1967) maintains that only where opposition is effective can it be regarded as an indication of democracy, and this effectiveness is manifested in the closeness of elections or in the frequency of defeats of incumbents.

The debate between Martin and Edelstein seems to be a remarkably sterile one. We may agree with Martin that the existence, or potential existence, of factions provides the executive with an awareness of the need to remain sensitive to membership wishes, government proceeding by a process of loose coalitions and soundings of opinion rather than the 'either/or' dichotomy of electional closeness. Equally we may take Edelstein's point that factions may exist for years without success. Both models suffer from the attempt to account for democracy primarily in terms of one single constraint.

Democracy and oligarchy?

Union democracy is a question of degree rather than of kind. The closeness of elections, the tolerance of factions, the existence of formal and informal channels whereby members wishes are conveyed to decision-makers, and perhaps the possibility of members voting with their feet as the ultimate constraint, may all be considered factors contributing to the degree of democracy. Any constraint on the ability of trade union leaders to impose their will on a reluctant membership, even the unofficial strike, may be interpreted as a factor promoting union democracy.

The formal, institutional aspects of government provide only a general framework within which the conflicts that result from the diversity of interests are resolved. Of equal, or greater, importance are the ways in which these interests are defined by the conflicting groups and the processes whereby they are resolved. There are potential sources of conflict between groups at every level within a trade union. This suggests that the 'leaders and followers' model of government which forms the basis of most theorising to date (even Hemingway's conflict approach) may not always be the most appropriate. Activists, or leadership of a sort, are distributed through all the levels of a trade union; shop stewards, local officers, executive bodies, delegate conferences can all claim to have an interest in the decision-making process. And what is often described as membership apathy towards union government may be merely a reflection of the way members perceive the relevance of the national leadership to their day-to-day activities, particularly where there exists a well-developed shop stewards' organisation.

In this sense the union is not democratic, in that control over decision-making is not unquestionably in the hands of the membership, the rank and file, the *demos*, but neither is it oligarchic, in that power is not concentrated in the hands of a few chief officers. Rather, power is distributed through the union so that different levels or

5

groups have some scope to make decisions over certain limited issues. Naturally, we would expect that this in itself will be a source of friction as these groups seek for themselves new areas of responsibility and control. Michels argued that decentralisation would result only in the creation of a number of smaller, competing oligarchies. This again seems excessively pessimistic, because unless we regard a union's delegate conference, or a shop stewards' committee, or indeed any collection of activists, as inherently oligarchic, the way power is distributed in a union must be seen as something different from both oligarchy and democracy. As in the other conflict models this form of government is pluralist, but the essential features are more adequately conveyed by the term 'polyarchic'; that is, a government in which there are a number of loci of power and decision-making, some party, some faction, some formal, some informal.

The next chapter elaborates the concept of trade union polyarchy. The model offers a way of looking at trade union government in terms of the forms of power and influence which the levels or groups can call upon in the day-to-day process of negotiating over decisions or decision-making, or in the situations when overt conflict emerges between levels.

2
Trade union polyarchy

Banks (1974) refers to all trade unions as polyarchies, that is, organisations in which there is a balance of power between the leaders and a minority of active participants. Theories of union government have placed great emphasis on the nature and extent of rank-and-file participation and the polyarchic model is no exception. According to Banks, the existence of active participants at lower levels than that of leadership reduces or even eliminates the tendency to oligarchy, but equally, he argues, the lack of participation of the remainder of the rank and file reduces the degree of representative democracy.

Though Banks' view is acceptable at a fairly general level, it should be borne in mind that trade unions differ considerably in their forms of government and thus in the scope which they allow active participants to exercise some control over union activities. Similarly, Banks probably overstates the 'passivity' of the rank and file, even in a polyarchic form of government. The rank and file is not an undifferentiated mass but is usually made up of many types of union member, not only in terms of occupational interest but also in terms of attitude to trade unionism. For example, Seidman *et al.* (1958) distinguished seven types of rank-and-file member: the ideological trade unionist (engaged in the class struggles), the good union man, the loyal but critical member, the crisis activist, the dually-oriented member, the card carrier, and the unwilling unionist. These differences may provoke different responses to union activities depending on the issue in question. Additionally, almost all union activities will involve the rank and file to some degree, particularly the various forms of industrial action. Those occupying leadership positions in the trade union will be influenced in their actions by what they perceive to be the preferences of at least large sections of the rank and file. Indeed, one of the problems with the democratic model of union government is the difficulty for leaders in interpreting the interests of the membership, given the different levels at which trade unions are involved, from workplace bargaining through to national economic policy-making.

It is important not to carry too far the equation of participation with any particular form of trade union government. Democracy, oligarchy and polyarchy refer to types of control structures, that is, the way in which control is distributed and exercised in a union. Participation refers to the ways in which members take on organisational roles and the energies that they put into those roles (Tannenbaum and Kahn, 1958: 50).

The argument of this book is that control over decision-making is distributed among a series of collectivities, usually of a hierarchical kind, so that lower-level collectivities possess some degree of autonomy in decision-making. This autonomy may derive from the union's constitution, as with the district committees in the AUEW, or may have developed as a form of union 'custom and practice' as with many shop stewards' organisations. In addition, checks and balances limit the extent to which higher-level collectivities can take decisions without regard to the lower levels of union activists.

Depending on the union, these collectivities are variously called workshop organisations of shop stewards, branches, district or local committees and councils, regional committees and councils, the national conference, and the Executive Council. The rank and file plays a major role in government since it may provide a base of support or power for many different collectivities. However, it may be external to the process of negotiation between the collectivities over areas of decision-making and over specific decisions, in the sense that it can shift its support from one collectivity to another. Collectivities in dispute with each other may need to cultivate, and appeal to, the rank and file to demonstrate its support for one collectivity rather than the other(s).

Trade union government therefore has two distinct, though related, aspects. The first is that each element may have some sphere in which it is autonomous; that is, in which it can take decisions without regard to the other elements. The second aspect is that each element can exercise some restraint over other elements where there is perceived to be a divergence of interests. Such a divergence of interests may, of course, concern the boundaries of the areas of decision-making which are to be regarded as autonomous, and the shared definitions of these autonomous areas may be changed over time. Such a divergence of interests is illustrated by Hemingway's discussion of the Bridgend busmen's dispute with the National Union of Railwaymen (NUR). Hemingway remarks that, 'It was abundantly clear that what was at stake was the question of who was going to exercise control over union policy on these two matters of one-man operations and deductions through the paybill . . .' (1978: 105). In this instance we find one collectivity, the Bridgend branch, in dispute with the national executive, another collectivity. Each collectivity contained its leaders or activists, that for the branch being 'the dynamic and charismatic personality of the Branch Secretary' (1978: 91).

Internal power struggles are, therefore, an important aspect of union life. The various trade union collectivities may be regarded as 'competing' with each other for control over certain areas of decision-making, or over certain decisions, within the framework of the democratic rules of the organisation (Van de Vall, 1970: 153).

Negotiated and arbitrated outcomes

These competitions tend to take two forms, producing two types of outcome. In the first form of competition the collectivities settle their differences between them, without any recourse to other agencies outside the negotiations. Decision-making is confined within the competitive arena and the outcome will be determined by each competitor's sources of authority (such as that conveyed by the union rule book) or other forms of power. The outcome produced by this form of competition can be referred to as a 'negotiated' outcome. For example, a union executive may attempt to gain a favourable outcome in a competition with a local committee or a shop stewards' organisation by using sanctions available under the union's constitution. Alternatively it may appeal to the principle of elected leadership or of trade union solidarity. Lipset *et al.* note how powerful is the solidarity principle in denying legitimacy to opposition within unions, and Lerner quotes a union leader faced by dissent: 'Loyalty is the highest form of discipline. It implies a readiness on the part of each one to subordinate individual views and opinions to the general will and the common purpose of the union . . .' (1961: 114). Such sources of legitimacy do not rest on appeals outside the negotiating arena and may thus be termed 'internal sources of legitimacy'.

Additionally, however, competition may take the form of an appeal for support directed to agencies outside the dispute, and in this form the recipients of those appeals determine the outcome of the competition. Support in this instance may be in the form of rank-and-file voting in elections, or compliance with one competitor's appeal as opposed to the appeal of the other. The unofficial strike, in which a plant membership supports its shop stewards against the appeals of a union executive represents a common form of this type of competition. In contrast with the negotiated outcome this latter form of competition may be said to produce an arbitrated outcome, and it is the arbiters who will grant legitimacy to one or other of the competitors. Appeals outside the negotiating arena are to 'external sources of legitimacy'. In this sense, the support which the arbiters give becomes a further source of power. These arbitrated outcomes are not necessarily the product of having the better case in a dispute, but may result from the nature of the formal and informal links that opposing parties have with those for whose support they are competing (Van de Vall, 1970: 230).

Within a trade union it is this immediacy of contact which has contributed to the growing ability of shop stewards' organisations to act independently of the trade union hierarchy. If a workshop group cannot accept the official leadership as legitimate they may transfer legitimacy permanently or temporarily to an unofficial leader. In his autobiography Jack Dash (1970), the unofficial London dockers' leader in the 1960s, describes how when the union was behaving in ways which the dockers rejected, the dockers withdrew legitimacy and transferred it to him and the group of shop stewards that he led. Yet on some issues, such as the demonstrations against coloured immigrants, he too was ignored in favour of other unofficial leaders. When this occurs, the competition between official and unofficial leaders is 'arbitrated' by the work group, the compliance with the demands or appeals of one of the groups being the manifestation of that arbitration.

In the most general sense, all disputes over the boundaries of decision-making are disputes over legitimacy: which collectivity shall have the authority to make decisions in any particular area. Lipset *et al.* examine the nature of legitimacy in the context of the legitimacy of opposition groups within a trade union. This is an important consideration in a 'leaders and followers' model of government but becomes less so when government is viewed as polyarchic. In a polyarchy all collectivities have some claim to legitimacy in limited areas, some well-defined and some ill-defined.

Contingent and non-contingent sources of legitimacy

In the arbitrated form of outcome it is possible to identify two major sources of external legitimation. Having defined polyarchy in terms of the relationship between active participants, probably the most important of these external sources is the passive membership, though the employers or employers' organisations can also be regarded as external sources of legitimation.

Legitimacy conferred by one external source is often dependent upon legitimacy being conferred by another. For example, the passive membership in the workshop may confer greater legitimacy on a collectivity that has been granted recognition (legitimacy) by the employers than on one that has not, particularly if the membership's orientation to the collectivity is primarily instrumental. Of the early days of the United Auto Workers Lipset *et al.* remark that 'Without having yet achieved legitimacy in their relations with management, the men who were in union office were unable to achieve the monopoly of political legitimacy internally that is the prerequisite of oligarchic control' (1956: 242). This type of legitimacy may be referred to as 'contingent legitimacy' since its conferment is conditional upon the other external source continuing to grant legitimacy. Legitimacy that is conferred in the absence of, or prior to, legitimation from another source would thus be termed 'non-contingent legitimacy'. This, for example, is the form of legitimation granted to union leaders on normative grounds during a union's struggles to gain recognition.

There is an inherent circularity in the relationship between contingent and non-contingent legitimacy, as is demonstrated by Bain (1972) in his discussion of white-collar unionism. He notes that the growth of union membership among white-collar workers is fastest where the employer recognises the union, particularly if for negotiating purposes, largely because 'unions are usually accepted on instrumental rather than ideological grounds' (1972: 259). But equally, Bain recognises, legitimation of the union by the employer may be dependent on the union securing support from a large enough proportion of the work-force. However, Bain argues that recognition by the employer has been the independent variable, in that rapid growth of union membership often follows recognition, whereas recognition less clearly follows rapid membership growth. In the white-collar case of instrumental rather than normative orientations to trade unionism the employer grants non-contingent legitimacy by recognition, whereas the subsequent support from the work-force takes the form of contingent legitimacy. The distinction between these two forms of legitimacy is important because it helps to explain the strategies and the processes in competitions between collectivities within a union. Many writers have argued that member orientations to trade unions are primarily instrumental, even though members sometimes regret this. Their support for one collectivity rather than another is likely to be based first on the strength of the linkages with the collectivities (which will determine the form and content of information about the conflict), and based secondly on which level of collective organisation is seen as most effective for the satisfaction of the goals which are most immediately pressing (Fox, 1971: 111).

A union collectivity may seek to build and maintain legitimation from one source in order to achieve legitimation from others. Each of the external sources of legitimacy (the passive membership and the employers) is capable of conferring or denying both contingent and non-contingent legitimacy in varying degrees.

External legitimacy and the rank and file

The rank-and-file member may exercise an arbitral role in a number of ways. For the most part the rank and file take a passive position with regard to union affairs, as in the distinction between active democracy (which involves high levels of direct participation in decision-making) and passive democracy (characteristic of demo-cracy dominated by electoral systems). Employing the concept of polyarchy, rather than democracy, the active members are those who participate directly in decision-making in each of the collectivities which make up the trade union. Most of these collectivities, such as the national executives, delegate conferences, district councils or committees and shop stewards' organisations, will be composed entirely of activists, so defined. Other collectivities, such as the branch and the workshop, will be composed of both active and passive members, as, of course, will be each trade union taken as a single collectivity.

It is the passive members who would take part in what Hoxie

referred to as the 'democratic uprising of the rank and file of the union' if the union 'failed to deliver the goods' (1923). It is in this sense that the passive members can act as arbiters of legitimacy since their behaviour will indicate support for one or other collectivity. Tannenbaum and Kahn (1958) suggest that the inactive membership possesses 'ratification power', and though inactive can therefore exercise control over decision-takers because of what they might or might not do. As distinct from this potential activity the mechanisms whereby legitimation becomes manifest depend upon the behavioural options open to the membership. Clearly, electoral behaviour will be limited by the frequency of elections and their relevance to the competition being arbitrated. The role of electoral behaviour will be most pronounced in factional competitions for specific union posts, but occasionally the electoral issues may centre around the legitimacy of different collectivities in the hierarchy. For example, in 1967 Hugh Scanlon fought and won the election for President of the AUEW on a platform of reducing executive control and giving more authority to local and regional collectivities.

Other than through electoral behaviour the membership may register their support through compliance with one collectivity's demands as opposed to those of another, or, in the extreme case, the membership may transfer legitimacy from one union to another. The wealth of examples of these forms of conflict make it possible to agree with Hemingway that conflict is a typical state of affairs and that bargaining represents the everyday process of government. Hemingway's case studies of the Bridgend busmen, the Seamen's Union, and the Insurance Agents indicate the ways in which these conflicts are manifest and the processes whereby they are pursued. In each of these cases activists at levels below that of the national leadership appealed to otherwise passive members of the union for support. This support was manifest in a number of ways. In the Seamen's Union and among the Insurance Agents the activists campaigned for electoral support. In the Bridgend busmen's dispute the branch members followed the policy of the branch secretary in defiance of the national leadership. In the Ford strike of 1969, General and Municipal Workers Union (GMWU) members transferred to the Transport and General Workers Union (TGWU) and the Amalgamated Union of Engineering and Foundry Workers (AEF). At Pilkingtons in 1970 some of the GMWU membership transferred legitimacy to the short-lived breakaway union, the Glass and

General Workers Union. Lerner (1961), examining the factors which caused groups to break away from their unions, concludes that disaffection develops when unions fail to maintain sufficient administrative elasticity to cater for the diversity of interests among a heterogeneous membership.

For many of these cases it might be argued that an oligarchic model of trade union government could cope as adequately as any other, since the members are primarily in conflict with the national leadership. Though activists and 'leaderships' are distributed throughout the union hierarchy, in these cases the thrust of the dissent is upwards and it is the national leaderships that constitute the main participants in the competition. However, this is not always the case. In the AUEW disputes have arisen between various combinations of shop stewards' organisations, district committees, branches and local officials, with the national leadership not intervening or adopting an ambivalent position. Batstone, Boraston and Frenkel note that: 'At least potentially, conflicts may exist between full-time officials and domestic organisations' (1977: 202) and similar findings are reported by Boraston, Clegg and Rimmer (1975). They noted several examples of plant organisations over whose activities the local district committee had no control. In Birmingham, conflicts have arisen between the full-time officials and branches in the transport trade group of the TGWU.

Thus it can be argued that though disputes with the national leadership represent a high proportion of conflicts within trade unions, they are only one aspect of the continuous process of competition. Although the passive membership enters into conflicts as an arbiter and gives the appearance of engaging in a democratic process, the struggle for power lies elsewhere.

External legitimacy and the employers

The importance of employer recognition in the creation of contingent legitimacy from instrumentally oriented members has been noted, particularly as elaborated by Bain with reference to white-collar workers. However, the implications of employer recognition go further in that the employer has great scope for recognising and legitimising employee collectivities other than that of the national leadership. Clegg (1976) suggests that the main influence on the hierarchical level of collective bargaining and the power and the

independence of workplace organisations is the structure of management and employers' organisations. Through their informal organisations and their willingness to bargain at different levels the
employers determine which collectivity they will bargain with, and
hence which element can use this position as a claim for the support of
the instrumentally oriented member. Management may enhance the
scope, power and authority of shop stewards, and create a nearly
continuous struggle for power and influence not only between
stewards and management but often between stewards and their
unions externally. If the employers legitimate shop stewards' organisations for bargaining purposes, contingent legitimacy will be conferred upon these organisations by the membership in the workshop or
plant. Because the employers can withdraw the legitimacy the shop
stewards may become concerned with safeguarding their relationship
with the management. In one sense all workshop organisations are
dependent on management. The stewards may compromise on how
far they can go in opposing management without damaging the
relationship (Walton and McKersie, 1965: 201) or modify the notion
of opposition altogether and promote the idea of collaboration with
management (Fox, 1971: 125). It may, of course, be such collaboration that brings a shop stewards' organisation into conflict with
other elements in the trade union, but as long as the members in the
workshop share the perceptions of the stewards' organisation,
contingent legitimacy is more likely to be conferred on the stewards.
Anything which strengthens a union in its dealing with management
is likely to enhance its authority over its own rank-and-file members,
and in the same way it can be argued that anything which strengthens
one collectivity in its dealings with management enhances its
authority, not only over the rank and file, but also over other
collectivities.

The employers may grant non-contingent legitimacy to different
trade union collectivities for a number of reasons. For example,
Goodman and Whittingham (1973) ascribe the historical preference
of employers for industry-wide bargaining to the advantages of
uniform claims, simultaneous stoppages and eliminating unfair
competition.

Lerner's case study of the secessions from the Post Office
Engineering Union indicates how important is employer legitimation
in a competition between rival collectivities, in this case an established trade union and a breakaway group, the Engineering

Officers (Telecommunications) Association. The breakaway union campaigned vigorously for recognition from the Post Office but when this was not forthcoming the union lost support and conceded defeat to the POEU.

Another example of the major role played by recognition in the attraction of members to breakaway or small unions is provided by the experience of the unions in the electricity supply industry. In 1966 a number of disaffected members of the manual workers' union formed the breakaway Electricity Supply Union (ESU). However, in 1969, this union failed to secure recognition when the Generating Board reached a recognition agreement with the TGWU, GMWU, AUEW and EETPU. Encouraged by the hope of recognition given by the 1971 Industrial Relations Act the ESU managed to increase its membership but when this Act was repealed, and recognition failed to materialise, the membership drifted away.

More recently the white-collar unions have faced similar problems when in 1977 the Engineering Managers Association (EMA) representing technicians and managers in the electricity supply industry tried to break into the mainstream of the engineering industry. The union gained recognition from the Board of British Shipbuilders in spite of a recognition agreement covering five other white-collar unions. The TUC Disputes Committee ruled that the recruiting policies of the EMA were contrary to the Bridlington Principles (designed to prevent poaching or incursion into another union's traditional recruiting areas) and told EMA (a TUC-affiliated union) to stop recruiting.

Up to August 1980 the Advisory Conciliation and Arbitration Service (ACAS) administered statutory recognition procedures, and the criteria that ACAS used for assessing recognition cases throw some important light on the chances of a breakaway union achieving long-term existence. The most important instance was the claim for recognition by the UK Association of Professional Engineers (UKAPE) at W. H. Allen Ltd. ACAS reasoned that the recognition of UKAPE would be prejudicial to the established collective bargaining arrangements and refused UKAPE recognition. Since any small union, or breakaway union, would disturb these arrangements, they could expect little support from the statutory process. In July 1978 the ACAS decision was overturned in the High Court, a judgement upheld by the Appeal Court in January 1979. However, in February 1980 the House of Lords ruled in favour of ACAS. From

Table 1 *Sources of power in a polyarchy*

Internal		External	
Legitimacy	Other	Legitimacy	Other
Rule book	Sanctions (positive and negative)	Employers	Employers (closed shop)
Electoral principle	Expertise/inter-dependence	Passive membership	Sanctions of higher-level collectivity
Solidarity principle			

the cases of the ESU, EMA and UKAPE there is little to suggest that small or breakaway trade unions are likely to find it easy to obtain employer recognition, particularly when opposed by the existing unions.

Legitimate authority and power in a polyarchy

The idea of legitimate authority being employed here is one of several bases of social power. In the same way as a distinction has been made between internal and external sources of legitimacy in a trade union it is possible to distinguish between internal and external sources of power. This broad-brush approach to the nature of power and authority, and indeed, related concepts such as influence or control, does less than justice to the considerable amount of work which has been done on power by other writers. At its simplest, the view taken here is that power is employed when decisions are made, while recognising that key decisions may be prevented from reaching the decision-making area (Bachrach and Baratz, 1962, 1963 and 1970) or that issues may be framed in such a way that one party's real interests are obscured (Lukes, 1974). Manifest conflict in trade unions is only one aspect of power, but where it occurs the processes of control are most clearly revealed.

In a competition between two hierarchical collectivities in a trade union, each collectivity can draw upon both internal and external sources of power, including legitimacy. The sources available are presented in Table 1.

The internal sources of power consist of legitimacy (described above as emanating from the rule book, the electoral principle and the solidarity principle) and other internal sources such as sanctions (positive and negative) and ties of exchange and inter-dependence. External sources of power consist of external legitimacy (contingent and non-contingent conferred by the employers and passive membership) and other external sources such as sanctions applicable by a higher-level collectivity, and employer sanctions through the closed shop. Fox emphasises that when a hierarchically superior collectivity can draw upon external sources of support it is in a very strong position in relation to the individual member. It is only a minor extension of this argument to see that a collectivity which is fully recognised, has a closed shop and participates in joint agreements which successfully regulate terms and conditions of employment (Fox, 1971: 16) is in a strong position in relation to other collectivities as well.

Summary of the model

Voting, compliance and retention of membership are the three ways in which the passive membership can register their legitimation of one or other of the competing collectivities. Though the employers may confer contingent and non-contingent legitimacy on a collectivity and thus influence which collectivity receives the support of the instrumentally oriented member it is the passive membership that exercises the final arbitration of outcomes. Although the concept of polyarchy emphasises the relationships between collectivities, and the checks and balances of trade union government, these relationships do not exist in isolation from the union membership or from other institutions.

In the competitions implied by the concept of government, internal and external sources of power, particularly legitimacy, are called upon by the collectivities to gain control over specific decisions or over areas of decision-making. Unless these competitions prove to be schismatic they take place within the framework of rules of the organisation, a principle sometimes emphasised in trade unions by the existence of an appeals procedure or an appeals court to referee the competition and to interpret these rules.

Though other writers, such as Hemingway, have conceptualised trade union government in the form of a conflict model, they have retained the notion of government as embodying a leadership and membership dichotomy. The value of the little-explored view that trade union governments are polyarchies is that it recognises the plurality of collectivities within trade unions, each of which contains leaders and followers. As leadership is distributed throughout the trade union, then so too is government. Conflict can thus be understood as the outcome of competing claims to have legitimate control over individual decisions or whole areas of decision-making.

Hemingway argues that 'the process of bargaining will determine whether leaders or members have their way' (1978: 177). The polyarchic model, too, emphasises the process of bargaining, but between leaders and leaders, collectivity versus collectivity, with the passive membership exercising an arbitral role through their action or inaction.

The model does not require that there is manifest conflict between collectivities. Indeed, it emphasises Hyman's point that these relationships are characterised by the negotiation of order in which 'reciprocal expectations, obligations and understandings develop' (1975: 163) but which may be disrupted.

Such a situation is rarely static. The power and influence of the different groups will change over time, and the basis of order must be constantly worked at. This highlights the importance of bargaining, important in any organisation, but critical to the workings of a pluralist society like a trade union.

3
Polyarchy in the engineering section of the AUEW

Introduction

With nearly one and a half million members (over a million in the Engineering section alone) the AUEW is the second largest trade union in Britain and as such occupies a central place in the trade union and labour movement of the country. The block voting system at the Trades Union Congress and Labour Party conferences ensures that the AUEW has an important say in the formation of industrial and political policies. It was the Engineers' vote which swung the TUC Conference in 1971 towards instructing unions not to register under the provisions of the Industrial Relations Act. At the Labour Party Conference about 90 per cent of the votes cast came from the trade unions and over half of these block votes came from the five largest unions.

Seats on the General Council of the TUC, the National Executive Committee of the Labour Party, and on bodies such as the National Economic Development Council provide the union with a further base from which to make its policies heard. The question of how these policies are arrived at is therefore of interest to more than just those concerned with trade union government.

Development of the union structure

The extent to which a union's structure allows scope for decentralisation in decision-making can usually, though not always, be explained by reference to the form of government adopted by the union during its formative years.

The current AUEW has developed out of a series of amalgamations the first phase of which culminated in the formation of the Amalgamated Society of Engineers (ASE) in 1851. These amalgamations between local craft associations set the pattern for the district organisation of the early ASE and created tensions between district autonomy and centralised direction which have persisted to the present day. The ASE was a union of skilled craftsmen, and the antibureaucratic character of the craft ethic engendered a resistance to control or supervision, not only by the employer but even by the union hierarchy.

Silverman (1970) has argued that organisations are shaped according to the predominant values of the society in which they are rooted, and whether or not one accepts this argument as being generally applicable to all organisations, it is evident that the founders of the nineteenth-century craft associations modelled their constitutions on the emerging political ideology of pluralism and representative democracy. Wary of the possibility of creating self-perpetuating oligarchies they built into these constitutions considerable checks and balances on the exercise of power by the leadership. In the remodelling of the ASE in 1892 (an important model for other craft associations) so far did this concern extend that they adopted a system of elected full-time officials in addition to an elected full-time Executive Council.

More checks and balances were built into the constitution in 1921 when a further amalgamation created the Amalgamated Engineering Union. As the dominant party to this merger the ASE's constitution was carried forward for the new union but in addition a National Committee was established to form union policy at an annual meeting. The initial attempt to devise a form of organisation that would give effective centralised leadership while allowing for a high degree of self-government in the localities has evolved into a form of government where 'central authority has been dispersed to a point at which it sometimes seems to disappear' (Turner, 1962: 225).

In 1926 the union was opened to all males in the engineering industry regardless of skill, and in 1943 women were admitted for the first time. But the basic structure and procedures have remained the same since 1921; the 1967 merger with the Amalgamated Union of Foundry Workers to form the Amalgamated Union of Engineering and Foundry Workers (AEF) and the 1971 merger with the Construction Engineering Union and the Draughtsmen and Allied Technicians Association to form the AUEW resulted in a sectionalised union, each section retaining its previous constitution. The constitution of the engineering section of the AUEW (the AUEW(E)

21

with which this book is concerned) thus derives from the constitution of the earlier craft associations, though now only about a quarter of the members belong to the skilled sections of the union.

Current organisation

The organisation of the AUEW(E) is shown in Figures 1 and 2. The AUEW(E) has over a million members in 2,626 branches organised into 203 districts. These districts are in turn organised into 26 divisions each of which sends two members to the annual National Committee meeting. The Executive Council is elected from seven Executive Council regions, and in addition there are other full-time officers elected from a constituency which corresponds to their area of responsibility. There is a separate, directly elected, appeal court of lay members, which is responsible for interpretation of the rules.

At district level the elected district committees are given considerable scope under union rules to pass resolutions on trade questions which, with agreement of the Executive Council, become binding on members in the district. In addition, these committees authorise the appointment of shop stewards and supervise their activities. Great independence has been ascribed to the district committees even from within the AUEW. Richter quotes a National Officer of the union as saying; 'We can't order the Districts to do anything; that is the trouble. So we just have to be satisfied with what we can get out of them' (1973: 77).

It is often noted that the AUEW(E) constitution embodies the same principle of separation of powers as the constitution of the United States; the legislature is the National Committee, the administration is the Executive Council and the judiciary is the Final Appeal Court. Though the constitution would appear to provide the basis for a model democratic union what has emerged is rather different. In some respects the union approaches the two-party system described by Lipset *et al.* Over the post-war period elections have been contested between 'moderates' and 'militants', with the practice of each 'party' nominating a single candidate for a post quite common. The militant section of the union secured its greatest gain with the election of Hugh Scanlon to President in 1967. Since then the fortunes of the militants have been in decline, such that by 1980 there were no Executive Council Officers who would normally be identified with the militant wing.

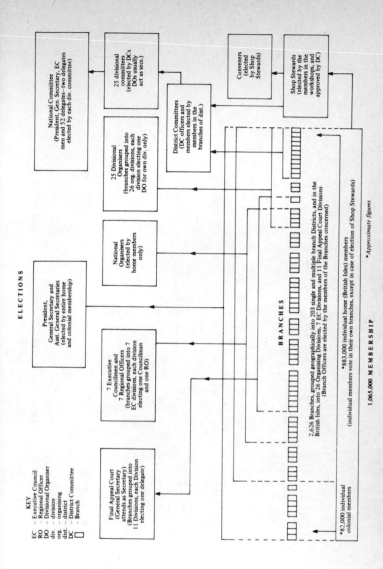

ELECTIONS

KEY

EC — Executive Council
RO — Regional Officer
DO — Divisional Organiser
div. — division
org. — organising
dist. — district
DC — District Committee
☐ — Branch

National Committee
(President, Gen. Secretary, EC
men and 52 delegates—two delegates
elected by each div. committee)

25 divisional committees
(elected by DCs
DOs usually
act as secs.)

Conveners
(elected
by Shop
Stewards)

Shop Stewards
(elected by the
members in the
workshops, and
approved by DC)

District Committees
(DC officers and
members elected by
members in the
branches of dist.)

25 Divisional Organisers
(branches grouped into
26 org. divisions, each
division electing one
DO for own div. only)

President, General Secretary and Asst. General Secretaries
(elected by entire home
and colonial membership)

National Organisers
(elected by
home members
only)

7 Executive Councilmen and 7 Regional Officers
(branches grouped into 7
EC divisions, each division
electing one Councilman
and one RO)

Final Appeal Court
(General Secretary)
attends as Secretary)
(Branches grouped into
11 Divisions, each Division
electing one delegate)

BRANCHES

2,626 Branches, grouped geographically into 203 single and multiple branch Districts, and in the
British Isles, into 26 Organising Divisions, 7 EC Divisions, and 11 Final Appeal Court Divisions
(Branch Officers are elected by the members of the Branches concerned)

1,065,000 MEMBERSHIP

*883,000 individual home (British Isles) members

(individual members vote in their own branches, except in case of election of Shop Stewards)

*82,000 individual
colonial members

*Approximate figures

Figure 1 The electoral system of the engineering section of the AUEW. *Source*: union records.

23

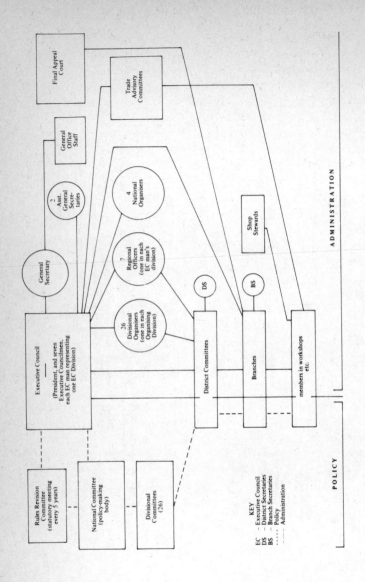

Figure 2 The formal policy-making and administrative organisation of the engineering section of the AUEW. *Source*: union records.

In that these factional conflicts cannot be terminated from the top the union conforms to the model of democracy proposed by Martin; in that the party system has tended to produce close elections it conforms to the model proposed by Edelstein. According to each of these measures (constitution, tolerance of factions, electoral closeness) the AUEW(E) is a model of democracy. Yet even a casual scrutiny of the internal workings of the union reveal it to be simultaneously characterised by conflict and by apathy. The preceding discussion has provided some clues as to why this should be and the remainder of the book will be concerned with an elaboration of the divergence between the predictions of the existing models of union government and the reality of internal political life in the AUEW(E).

The organisation charts merely indicate the formal lines of control in both policy-making and policy implementation. They show, for example, how the National Committee is indirectly elected via the branches and district and divisional committees, but not the rules which govern the relationship between the National Committee and the Executive Council. They show the dominant role of elections in the appointment of committees, councils and full-time officers, but not how often or how closely these elections are contested and how they might thus operate as a check on the exercise of power.

In order to consider these issues fully it is necessary to consider in turn each of the key elements in the organisation, always bearing in mind that such isolation is necessarily artificial since each element can only be fully understood in the context of all other elements.

Since it was with the local or regional organisations that the initial impetus of the union lay, the analysis begins by considering the evolution of the role of the district in the organisation.

The district

With the formation of the ASE in 1851, the predominant role of district bargaining in the 'Old Mechanics' (the Machine Makers Friendly Society, one of the most important of the societies in the amalgamation) was reflected in the creation of district committees to offset the central leadership of a London-based Executive Council. During the latter half of the nineteenth century the district was the focus of decision-making in the organisation. In the words of the union's historian:

The development of direct demands on the employers for increases in wages and the growth of local employers' associations increased the importance of district committees. It was the district committee men, meeting after a long day's work in the factory, who were responsible for choosing the right moment for wage demands, formulating the policy and negotiating with the employers. On their ability and energy depended to a large extent the advances made by the membership. The Executive sitting in London surveyed the wage developments throughout the country but except in cases when assistance was requested did little to sponsor wage movements. The increased influence of district committees led to uniformity of wages in each district by itself but the varying strengths of these committees and the uneven cost of living throughout the country led to marked variations in the district rates established. (J. B. Jefferys, 1946: 99)

From the end of the nineteenth century the role of the district in collective bargaining began to decline as both national and workshop bargaining increased in importance. In 1892 the great disparity between the district rates finally impelled the union to accept the necessity for some permanent central policy-making and executive body. Two proposals were put forward at the Leeds Delegate Meeting of 1892, one for a full-time elected committee, the other for an elected full-time staff of officials. Though these proposals were probably intended as alternatives, both were adopted. The old London-based Executive Council (composed exclusively since 1857 of working representatives of London branches) was replaced by an Executive Council consisting of full-time officials elected by eight electoral divisions.[1] At the district level, six full-time organising district delegates were to be elected to act as organisers, negotiators and intermediaries between the Executive Council and district committees.

The district committees were given the powers to appoint shop stewards and though Cole (1973) makes the point quite strongly that these early stewards only acted as agents of the district committee, Jefferys notes that they very quickly developed a semi-independent role for themselves. Cole maintains that before the First World War:

it was for the Union district as a whole, rather than for its representatives in any particular works, to deal with grievances when they arose, and the function of the works representatives was limited to the reporting of any difficulty arising, in order that the District Committee and officials might have the necessary data on which to take action. (1973: 10)

However, Jefferys writes that in the districts recognising piecework there was some confusion as to whether district committees or the newly forming shop committees were responsible for the control of prices.

The formation of the full-time Executive Council in 1851, and the growth in the number of shop stewards in the latter half of the nineteenth century signalled the decline of the district's role, though this decline was both gradual and occasionally resisted. After the dispute of 1897, in which the Engineering Employers 'locked out' the workers and succeeded in defeating the union, a new procedural agreement termed 'Provisions for the Avoidance of Disputes' laid down a disputes procedure which culminated in a national meeting between the Executive Board of the Employers Federation and the central authority of the trade union concerned. The Executive Council of the ASE decided to exclude local officials from the national negotiations arising from the procedure, a move which, Jefferys observes, was 'a severe blow to the local spirit and practice of the Society' (1946: 151).

However, the 'Terms of Settlement' of 1898 envisaged that collective agreements, as was normal practice at that time, would continue to be negotiated mainly on a district basis. This meant that though wages and hours were negotiated district by district, a dispute in any part of the country was liable to be taken to a *national* conference.

The existence of a national disputes procedure operating in parallel with local wage bargaining highlighted the organisational strains created by the divergence between the principles of centralised authority and local autonomy. In 1906 and 1907 the Manchester and Erith district committees were suspended for refusing to accept Executive Council recommendations following from national conferences. In 1908 the refusal of men on the north-east coast to accept Executive Council policy led to the resignation of the General

Secretary. In 1910 J. T. Brownlie (later Chairman of the ASE and President of the AEU) wrote in the *Monthly Journal* of the ASE: 'The most unpopular body within our borders is the Executive Council' (Jefferys, 1946: 169).

The society weathered this internal dissension and by the beginning of the First World War the only change in the organisation was the provision of full-time secretaries in the largest districts. The First World War accelerated the growth of both industry-wide and workshop bargaining. A Committee of Production was appointed by the government to determine wage awards in the engineering industry, and rather than persist with the lengthy routine of individual district applications agreement was reached in 1917 to suspend these and to replace them with general wage claims every four months.

By the end of the First World War industry-wide agreements on pay and hours of work were characteristic of the engineering industry. Though the separate district agreements were dying away the district's position in the constitution remained as before. However, this does not mean that after 1918 minimum wages were the same in all districts. This did not occur until 1968 as a result of the 1965 Package Agreement (AEU records).

That the period after 1918 did not see a reversion to district bargaining may be ascribed to the advantages that national bargaining gave to the unions and employers. The unions were able to conserve their resources, conduct negotiations through the most experienced officials, and more easily defend a national standard rather than district rates during periods of unemployment. For the employers, national negotiations meant that relative competitive positions would remain unchanged, while no one employer would be strike-bound when his competitors could continue to produce.

Although the greatest shift from district to national bargaining occurred in this period between the wars it was the First World War that 'broke fresh ground in establishing new national agreements' (Marsh, 1965: 146). So great was the change in emphasis during the war period that when the Whitley Committee debated what improvements could be made in the relations between employers and workers it assumed, almost without discussion, that organisation for negotiations and consultation would be industry-wide.

The decline of the district should not be overstated. What has been described is a change from a position of pre-eminence in the union to one where it plays an important, but diminished, part in union government. The traditions of local autonomy and the constitutional provisions (which may be described as a legacy of this autonomy) combine to give the district considerable scope in which to exercise control, though the precise nature of this control depends, as will be seen, on a configuration of other key variables.

District committee representatives are elected annually by the branches on the basis of one representative for every two branches up to a maximum of thirty branch representatives where the district has more than seventy branches. The representatives are elected at branch meetings in June and December, half being elected for twelve months from June to the following May and the other half for the twelve months from December to the following November. In addition, shop stewards are directly represented on the committee on the basis of one representative for every 5,000 members in the district. The shop stewards' representatives are elected for one-year periods at the December quarterly meeting of shop stewards. Since, almost by definition, district committees are composed of union activists, most of the representatives that come from the branches are also shop stewards, a point noted by the Donovan Commission in its criticism of the district committees: 'These powers [of the district committee to obstruct reform] come from two sources: the tradition of regulating work practices on a district basis; and the constitution of the district committee which tends to make it a coalition of representatives of the most powerful groups of stewards in the district' (1968: 42). The National Board for Prices and Incomes similarly considered that tradition played an important part in defining the current role of district committees: 'The powers of these district committees derive from the nineteenth century when wages and conditions were settled separately in each district. They are ill-suited to a time in which negotiations are generally by industry, by company, or by plant' (1967: 28), and Clegg concurs: 'The district committees may also use their powers to obstruct agreement between national union officers and individual companies . . . Nevertheless district powers have not been curtailed' (1970: 115).

As will be seen, such criticisms seriously overstate the powers of the district committees, and in focusing on the roles played by tradition and constitution obscure the mechanisms which define the powers of any particular committee. In the formal sense, at least, some of these powers derive from the rules of the union and in particular from Rule

12 which governs the activities of district committees (AUEW, 1980: 21–7).

Under the rules the district committees are the bodies which have the responsibility for authorising the appointment of shop stewards, defining their role, and supervising their activities. Similarly, they have the power to 'deal with and regulate rates of wages, hours of labour, terms of overtime, piecework and general conditions affecting the interests of the trades in their respective districts' (1980: 24).

According to Roberts (1956) the Executive Council has limited powers of supervision over the work of a district committee. However, all of the powers given to committees by the rules are subject to the proviso 'with the approval of the Executive Council'. Roberts sees as emphasising district committee authority the clause in Rule 14 which states that the Executive Council shall not complete an agreement with an employer without submitting the terms first to the district(s) affected, any dispute being referred to the National Committee. Though built into the rules as a check on the powers of the central authority this clause is rarely, if ever, used.

The district committee can take a ballot of their members on the advisability of a district strike and can declare such a strike if it has been supported by a three-to-two majority of the members voting. The committee can also approve shop or factory strikes within their district and where such approval has been given can conduct a ballot of their members on the advisability of levying a special strike fund. Arnison's (1970) study of the Roberts-Arundel dispute in 1966 provides a good example of the district strike fund in operation. When the management of Roberts-Arundel, a textile machinery company, locked out workers from the Stockport factory the district secretaries in the Ashton and Manchester districts organised a ballot in each district which resulted in all members paying a weekly levy of 6d to the strike fund.

Thus under rule the district committees are given powers over three important areas of union activity: the appointment and control of shop stewards, the conduct of negotiations on trade questions, and the initial sanctioning of strikes.

The Executive Council

It was to the Executive Council that early powers of the district first shifted, and much of the concern over the issue of central authority versus local autonomy can be reduced to a conflict between the Executive Council and district committes. The rules now embody the principle that the activities of all members (including district committees) are subject to the approval of the Executive Council, and in support of this principle sanctions are available under Rule 21. The role of the Council is intended to be primarily administrative rather than policy-making, however. Each of the seven members is elected for first a three-year, and then a five-year period and sits on the Executive Council full-time. The Council meets each week and this, together with its small size and full-time nature, allows ample scope for surveying activities in the union. Though it stands at the apex of the organisational system its power is subject to a number of checks. Apart from the possibility of individual members losing in an election, its decisions may be challenged in the Final Appeal Court. In addition, it is required under rule to follow the policy laid down for it by the annual National Committee meeting, though there is considerable latitude for interpretation of policy and little that can be done by the National Committee if its policy is not pursued. The extent to which the Executive Council follows National Committee policy depends in part upon the extent to which it wants to, as may be seen by the sharp difference between the administrations of Lord Carron and Hugh Scanlon. Lord Carron's repeated defiance of the National Committee become known as Carron's Law, whereas Hugh Scanlon took up an explicit position that National Committee policy would be followed. Roberts' suggestion that 'the executive council is not infrequently prevented from pursuing a wise policy by the powerful national committee' (1956: 156) is rather too strong. However, he may be correct in arguing that in those unions that have no national conferences the Executive Council 'may behave more ruthlessly than they would otherwise have' (1956: 158). Allen also notes that in those unions that have delegated their policy-making function to their Executive Councils 'these are the most authoritarian of executive councils' since 'a policy-forming executive is free from the restraint which a delegate assembly, conscious of its power, can impose' (1954: 172, 173). The Executive Councils of the steel unions, for example, carry a degree of authority possessed by few other unions, and the structures of both the large general unions create a degree of centralisation far greater than in the AUEW(E).

The National Committee

The delegate conference of the engineering section consists of the annual meeting[2] of the National Committee which was set up in 1921 at the formation of the AEU as a solution to the problem of centralising policy-making. As the previous discussion indicated, its relationships with the Executive Council (to whom its resolutions stand as instructions) have not always been unambiguous, the two bodies diverging considerably during the presidency of Lord Carron.

Each of the twenty-six divisional committees elects two representatives to the National Committee, and from 1949 to 1967 an additional seven union delegates were elected by the annual women's conference.

The divisional committee members are elected from the district committees which are in turn elected from the branches and shop stewards' quarterly meetings. Representation on the National Committee is indirect, a point referred to by Lord Carron in his address to the National Committee in 1961. On the basis of indirect election, Carron suggested, the National Committee delegates had the positive approval of only 4 per cent of the membership. 'How far', he asked, 'is the representative able to commit his electorate and be secure in the knowledge of full support and full approval by that electorate?'[3]

In his speech to the National Committee in 1953 the President, Jack Tanner, criticised delegates for voting according to the mandate of their divisional committee, 'not always because they really believed it [a resolution] sensible and practicable'.[4]

Tatlow (1953: 258) has suggested that the system of indirect elections helps a minority rise to power. 'The national committee', she argues, 'exercises power rather than responsibility.' Speeches, she goes on, 'are spattered with slogans of earlier struggles', the delegates speaking, 'with an eye to their constituency'.

Not only is its 'representativeness' questionable but so also is its role as a deliberative assembly. In common with the delegate conferences of other unions it is subject to the criticisms made by Allen (1954) that it may be swayed by oratory, or at the other extreme, delegates may be mandated by their divisional committees. Deliberation is further limited by the volume of resolutions it is required to consider. For example in 1968, 575 resolutions were forwarded to the committee, of which only 65 were adopted.

Richter (1973) has argued that the functional role of the National

Committee is now minimal. Its authority in collective bargaining has diminished with the shift to workshop or plant bargaining, and even in national bargaining the Committee plays no role in negotiations once these are in progress. However, under the presidency of Hugh Scanlon the National Committee passed resolutions on wage bargaining which were accepted as union policy.

In many ways it is better placed than the large delegate conferences of other unions and, as previously noted, 'all decisions of the national committee shall be final and binding on the executive council' (AUEW, 1980: 29).

Its role is limited by the infrequency of its meeting compared with the continuous policy implementation of the Executive Council and full-time officers. However, the Committee can hold 'recall' conferences to vote on policy issues (such as wage negotiations). A further important function for the National Committee is that every five years, after policy business has been dealt with, the Committee sits as a Rules Revision Committee. At this meeting all full-time officers except the President and General Secretary are excluded, though the Executive Council is permitted to submit suggestions for the revision of rules. As with the policy-making role, the National Committee can call a Rules Revision meeting at any time to consider suggestions by the Executive Council for rule changes.

Given the importance of the rule book in internal legitimation, and the 'legalistic' attitude to the rules in most trade unions, this rule-making capacity represents an important feature of the National Committee's role in the polyarchy.

The Final Appeal Court

If the National Committee may be likened to a legislature and the Executive Council to an administration so the Final Appeal Court may be seen as a judiciary, completing the analogy with the form of separation of powers found in national constitutions such as that of the United States. This Appeal Court consists of eleven members elected from the branches divided for the purpose into eleven electoral divisions, and it meets annually. Its role may be seen primarily as a check on the powers of the Executive Council since appeals are lodged against Executive Council decisions. However, this interpretation is misleading since the Executive Council is involved in Final Appeal Court deliberations partly because it is itself part of the judicial machinery. A complaint by a member against a district committee or a full-time official goes to the Executive Council for resolution. If both parties agree to the Executive's ruling no further action is necessary. If either party should disagree (not necessarily the original complainant) then the Executive's decision may be challenged in the Final Appeal Court. Hence, though the Appeal Court is ultimately a check on Executive authority, actual cases considered may be occasioned by disputes in other parts of the union.

The full-time officers

Though the seven members of the Executive Council are elected to serve full-time, this section is more concerned with the role of the other full-time officers, particularly at the local level. The AUEW(E) has approximately 188 full-time officials (the number of full-time district secretaries and assistant divisional organisers varies). In addition to the President and General Secretary there are two assistant general secretaries, seven national organisers, seven regional officers, twenty-six divisional organisers, twenty-one assistant divisional organisers and approximately 123 district secretaries. All are elected for initially three-year and subsequently five-year terms of office, the constituency of the President, the General Secretary, his assistants, and the national organisers being the entire membership, the constituencies of the remainder corresponding to their geographical responsibilities.

Under rule, all the full-time officers, with the exception of the President and District Secretaries, are held to be responsible to the Executive Council. Their responsibilities are organising and administrative, but this freedom to act is limited by their formal responsibilities to the Executive Council and district committees, and by the informal sanction of electoral loss of office. In the AUEW(E), election results are sufficiently close to indicate that the electoral sanction is a real one, and to win elections the full-time officials need the support of district committees and the stewards in large plants.

Not only must the officials consider the electoral consequences of their actions but also whether their actions will be ratified by the relevant committee or council. For example, the role of Divisional Organisers is limited by their relationship with the district committees:

Organisers shall, when requested by any district committee in their division, conduct negotiations with employers in the district in which they are located. They shall report to the district secretary on arriving and leaving the town in which they are located. They must act in conjunction with the secretary or other member appointed by the respective committee with whom they are for the time being connected, and shall not, under any circumstances, conclude on their own authority any arrangement that will alter or affect any of the recognised conditions of the district committee within the area in which they may be acting. They shall act at the request of any district committee, or attend, without payment, any district meeting, when deemed necessary, but under no circumstances shall they enter into any negotiations in any district without the consent of the committee of such district. (AUEW, 1980: 41)

Similarly, the work of the District Secretary is subject to ratification by his committee.

These provisions contrast sharply with the powers of full-time officers in other unions. In the GMWU for example, it is highly unlikely that the district committee would try to change the decision of a district officer, but the AUEW national officials are indirectly subject to the policies of the elected National Committee and local officials can rarely settle with an employer without reference back to the district committee. Whereas officials in the AUEW are subject to keenly fought elections, officials in the GMWU are not subject to periodic re-election. Though the GMWU has worked towards constitutional reform in the 1970s the force of Lane and Roberts' (1971) comments remain:

What emerges from all this is that there is a distinctly professional aroma about the GMWU – that is to say effectively it regards its members as clients rather than as participants. The 'members' pay their dues and in return are provided with certain services – provided they do as they are told. A very distinct line is drawn between the union and its members – the union becomes the organisation, its corps of full-time officials. The members become passive duespayers who may be allowed a vote now and again (but they can only vote for people approved of by the 'union') and to send delegates to a conference which effectively has very little power. The union is in other words very much in the charge of its officials, officials over whom the lay membership has little control since they are not subject to periodic re-election. (1971: 55)

Shop stewards

The well documented growth of plant and workshop bargaining and the parallel growth in the role and numbers of shop stewards have given rise to an important element in the nature of government in the AUEW. In 1960 the union had 23,500 shop stewards, 26,600 in 1965, 34,000 in 1973, and 40,000 in 1981. Though they are represented on the district committee directly through the shop stewards' quarterly meeting and indirectly through branch elections, the integration of the stewards into union government is far from complete. There is thus a tendency for stewards to work outside the formal structure of the union through shop stewards' committees both within and between plants. The shop steward 'problem' has been a feature of the unions' internal life almost as important as the tension between district autonomy and national bargaining.

In 1961 the *Guardian* reported:

> Leaders of the AEU took further steps to discipline unruly shop stewards. After the threat last week to expel members who persisted in the unofficial strike at the British Light Steel Pressings factory at Acton, a letter was sent yesterday to the AEU District Secretary in North London ordering him to provide the names of shop stewards leading the dispute. The men – about ten are thought to be involved – will probably be summoned to union headquarters for disciplinary action. British Light Steel Pressings has been a trouble spot, standing out even in the troublesome North London district of the AEU, in which the national leadership has had difficulty in keeping local officials under control. During the present strike shop stewards are said to have prevented a national officer from addressing the strikers.[5]

The existence of unofficial shop stewards' movements such as the Engineering and Allied Trades National Council of Shop Stewards has created further difficulties for the Executive Council. Though this body was defunct by the mid-1960s the evidence of newspaper reports, Executive Council circulars, and articles in the Union's *Monthly Journal*, suggests that the problem of controlling shop stewards did not die with it. As Turner argued, such unofficial shop stewards' organisations may provide 'a kind of immanent alternative leadership of engineering workers' (1950: 187).

Shop stewards have undoubtedly acquired much of their powers as a result of the growth of plant bargaining in the engineering industry. Unlike the committees, councils, and officers discussed so far, the steward derives little authority from the union rule book. Plant bargaining, however, confers an authority which can be used to influence union decisions, both informally through shop steward pressure groups and formally through representation on committees and councils. In addition, they may derive power from their ability to influence electoral outcomes, but ultimately their authority is derived from the work groups which they represent, particularly the willingness of work groups to follow their direction.

The branch

Just as well documented as the rise of the shop steward is the decline of the branch. In the AUEW(E) branches are geographically organised and form the basis of organisation. As with other unions, attendances are very low even though under rule each member is required to attend the branch to pay subscriptions and to vote in elections for some posts and delegate positions. In practice subscriptions are collected either by stewards or by a check-off agreement, whereby members' union contributions are deducted from pay by the employer and passed directly to the union. Even when subscriptions are paid at the branch the member may attend briefly for this one purpose. Similarly, the change to postal balloting for general officers in 1972 has removed one of the few remaining motives for branch attendance. As Jim Conway suggested when General Secretary: 'We all know that in the main branch life is dead. Our voting returns for elections confirm this fact. The seat of activity is in the factory.'[6] Similarly, George Woodcock once remarked: 'Branches have ceased to be an important part of trade union structure. Trade union activity takes place at the place of work in the shop. If I were an active trade unionist again, you would not find me anywhere near a branch because there is not enough done to justify attendance' (Cyriax and Oakeshott, 1960: 69).

Polyarchy

As the discussion of the key elements in the union has shown, control over decisions is fairly equally distributed between the shop stewards, the district committees, the Executive Council, the National Committee, and, to a lesser extent, the full-time officers. The branch performs a mainly administrative function, the divisional committees forward resolutions to the National Committee and the role of the Final Appeal Court is that of arbitration.

The structure, with its complex system of checks and balances has aroused a great deal of criticism. Turner noted with particular reference to the district, that the parallel existence of elected officials and elected representatives creates confusion as to where authority and responsibility lie (1950: 183). Fay maintains that the AUEW(E) is more like a *laissez-faire* control structure than polyarchic: 'It [the AEF, writing in 1970] is riddled with the excesses of democracy . . . It is a tortuous system designed to produce maximum rank-and-file control, which gives no-one control' (1970: 62). This would appear to overstate considerably the degree of rank-and-file control intended in the system, though it is a view often expressed from within the union itself. During the Donovan Commission hearings, Lord Carron (then President of the AEU) agreed with Lord Tangley's point that:

> I may be wrong but it seems to me that in your union
> the power flows from the bottom up, in the sense that the
> branches have the real power and the powers of the
> district derive from the branches, the powers of the
> division derive from the district and the powers of the
> national organisation derive from below, and most of the
> officers are subject to election by the required form at
> various levels. This seems to suggest that in fact the real
> seat of power is in the branch, and persuasion flows
> downwards from the top: is that right? (AEU, 1968: 987)

Again, this greatly overstates the powers of the branch and understates that of the executive.

The power and control relations between the various parts of the union may much more sensibly be understood with reference to Tannenbaum's (1968) concept of polyarchic control. The essence of Tannenbaum's concept of control (which he defines synonymously with power), is that effective control requires that some be exercised by all participants so that the total amount within an organisation is expanded. Granting to rank-and-file members the opportunity to participate directly or indirectly in decision-making increases the willingness to implement decisions and thus the amount of control at all levels. This is not the same thing as 'democracy', which carries the implication that rank-and-file control is achieved at the expense of the leadership's control, nor 'autocracy', where leadership control is acquired at the expense of rank-and-file control. Though all unions may be polyarchies as Banks suggests, not all embody the principle to the same degree. Fay argued, for example: 'The GMWU offers an intriguing contrast to the AEF since its leadership is constitutionally powerful, but its rank and file seems to lack independence, guts even' (1970: 67).

Fox characterises trade unions as 'a number of collectivities structured into a hierarchy culminating in the national level of the union' in which 'groups with differing goals seek to use an organisation of power and resources and symbols in the service of their own interests' (1971: 110 and 114). The willingness of the parties to co-operate depends upon the extent to which co-operation advances these self-interests and enables each to achieve their desired objectives. The various 'power centres' are interdependent in any union but in the AUEW(E) the groups enjoy a relatively high degree of functional autonomy in their interrelationship. Their interactions take the form of continuous bargaining and the result is an inevitably imperfectly integrated system of control. The continued growth and survival of the union itself relies on a minimum set of common standards within which such bargaining takes place.

The analysis of control thus revolves around the notions of autonomy and interdependence, an approach explored by Boraston *et al.* (1975) in their study of district committees in the AUEW(E).

They argued that large plants would develop workshop organisations capable of accumulating resources such as experience, expertise, time and facilities and hence become independent of the district organisation. Several examples are quoted to illustrate the limitations thus imposed on the district committee's authority in the workshops.

Tannenbaum's concept of polyarchic control implies that legitimacy derived from participation in decision-making enables total control to be expanded, and thus control is not a zero-sum concept. Where legitimacy breaks down, however, bargaining between interest groups takes place and the successful outcomes of such bargaining for one group will normally be at the expense of another.

4

The Manchester district committee

Introduction: divison of the district

In May 1979 the Manchester district committee, on which this study is based, was divided into the districts of Manchester North and Manchester South. Pressure for such a division had been building up for some time. The old Manchester district had contained a membership of between thirty and thirty-five thousand members with over 600 stewards and 90 branches. Though the Birmingham district had nearly 54,000 members before division in 1965, and the Coventry district had over 40,000 members in 1970, at just over 30,000 members the Manchester district was one of the largest in the union. The problems that this size posed for representation and administration had led one branch to complain as early as 1959 that the District Secretary was prevented from servicing properly the members and shop stewards, and that it was difficult to find branch representatives to serve on the committee because of the problem of reporting back to three branches. At a special sub-committee held on 27 October 1959 those problems were discussed, but it was decided to apply for an Assistant Divisional Organiser rather than for the district to be divided.

However, by 1970, although the district membership was no larger, further pressure for division was applied. Bob Wright, Executive Council representative put the case for division:

> In considering the position regarding Manchester,
> Executive Council recognise that with a loss of industry
> in the heavy engineering sector, the growth of small
> factories and maintenance services who are organized in
> our Union, and the general pattern of the spread of
> industry, close regard must be established to the service

41

which these industries requires from the District Committee and the Secretary. Also, that the level of activity generated by Plant Bargaining, legislation, representations of members at Appeals Tribunals, Industrial Tribunals and other individual forms of liability, require that the Secretary should be able to cope adequately with such commitments. (From a copy of the statement made to the meeting of the committee)

The problems created by the size and occupational diversity of the membership in the district, which led to pressures for division, relate directly to the problems of control between the district committee and the branches, shop stewards and membership. As Bob Wright's statement indicates, the increase in the variety of demands placed upon the district organisation makes more difficult the adequate treatment of each demand and hence lowers the quality of the service which can be offered to the membership in the firms. Similarly, this variety, by weakening the linkages that the district organisation maintains with the membership in the plants, reduces the ability of the district organisation to monitor the activities in those plants. Even so, it was not until 1979 that the division occurred.

The Manchester district was only one among a number of districts which covered the industrial area of South-east Lancashire and North Cheshire. Geographically, the district was not within a circle drawn from the centre of Manchester. On the East the boundaries with the Oldham and Stockport districts lay about four miles from the city centre, whereas in the West the district extended along the Manchester Ship Canal as far as Cadishead (about ten miles from the city centre). This placed the geographical centre of the district near to the present site of the district offices in Salford.

The area includes a great variety of industries, light and heavy, engineering and non-engineering. There are a number of large electrical engineering plants in the district (most notably AEI, Ferranti, and Ward and Goldstone), engineering firms such as Massey Ferguson, Renold Chains and Gardners, in addition to a Royal Ordnance Factory, a large petro-chemical site, and railway workshops.

The division was carried out by a neat splicing of the district on an east–west line drawn along the Manchester Ship Canal, the Mancunian Way, and the railway. The division produced two districts

Table 2 *Manchester district membership of the AUEW(E) 1950–81*

	Shop stewards	Branches	Membership
1950	664	85	33,597
1960	633	88	34,906
1970	710	91	32,528
1979 (at division)	650	80	28,000
1981 (south)	300	36	12,500
1981 (north)	300	36	12,500

Source: Official Union Records at Head Office, and district estimates. (Figures for 1979 and 1981 are estimates only.)

almost equal in geographical area, membership, shop stewards and branches. Table 2 shows the size of the district in the post-war years. The sharp decline in membership, branches and stewards from the late 1970s onwards was almost entirely the result of massive closures and redundancies in the district.

The structure of district committee membership

As Manchester was a district with more than 70 branches (about 90 between 1960 and 1970) the rules entitled the branches to have 30 representatives to the committee. In addition, the district's membership of 30,000–35,000 members entitled the committee to six or seven shop steward representatives (one for every 5,000 members in the district). A woman delegate and the District President brought the permitted size of the committee to just under 40 members.

The branch representatives on the committee were elected from 30 groupings of branches which meant that nearly all of the representatives would be elected from, and required to report back to, three branches. As noted earlier in the chapter, this led to problems in securing members willing to stand as branch representatives. The records show that during the 1960s there was no year in which fewer than four seats were unfilled, and in a number of years (1965, 1966, 1967) there were as many as six unfilled branch seats (or 20 per cent of the total available branch places). In addition, the minutes note that many of the branch representatives' seats were uncontested so that nominees were declared elected without voting taking place. The study of Boraston *et al.* also suggests that the elections for branch representatives are not keenly contested. They found that 'it seemed to be no great problem for a Convener, who had lost his seat as a shop stewards' representative, to regain it as a branch representative' (1975: 26). Since division, however, the position has improved. In 1981 both districts, for the first time in the current Secretary's experience (going back to 1947), had a full complement of members.

There is a difference, however, between the Manchester district and the district which Boraston *et al.* call 'Leachester' with regard to the election of shop stewards' representatives. In all districts these representatives are elected at the December quarterly meeting of shop stewards of that district. In the 'Leachester' district the authors report that 'the number of candidates seeking election as shop stewards' representatives usually exceeded thirty' and the process whereby they are elected is described as 'robust' (1975: 26). Though the number of available places in the Manchester district was the same (usually seven) the number of nominations rarely exceeded ten. Thus, although in the Manchester district the shop stewards' places on the committee are more keenly contested than the branch places, there is no evidence of the strong competition to sit on the district committee found in the 'Leachester' district.

The actual composition of the membership consisted of a core of about a dozen long-serving members supplemented by a fairly high turnover of shorter-serving members. For example, 13 of the members of the committee in 1970 had served for over five years, and over the period from 1945 to 1970, 21 committee members served for twelve or more years (and several for over twenty years). In contrast, of members joining after 1946 (but not including new members in 1969) 65 left after serving only one term, and 37 left after serving only two terms (excluding new members in 1968).

The fact that elections for the committee are not robust may severely weaken claims for legitimacy derived from the electoral process, particularly in competitions with other collectivities whose claim to electoral legitimacy may be as strong or stronger (for example, shop stewards or the Executive Council). In addition, the high turnover of committee members may weaken claims for expert power, since this is derived from experience and knowledge wider than that afforded by the individual plant. Nevertheless this weakness may be offset by the existence of an experienced core membership.

Within the committee itself this core may be expected to exercise a considerable say in the conduct of committee business. In the same way as control over decision-making between collectivities may be in part determined by critical resources of experience and expertise, so too within the committee would the longer-serving members be able to exercise greater control of committee decision-making. The newer members, with a lesser knowledge of precedents, previous agreements, earlier disputes, or current agreements, would become involved in a learning process before entering fully into committee decision-making. The felt inexperience and lack of confidence of newly-elected representatives when faced with what appears to be an expert core tends to militate against an immediate involvement in decision-making. In particular, the experience of the core may carry the greatest weight in defining what is possible in terms of committee actions.

Length of experience provides one structural dimension on which to examine committee leadership. Another dimension is that of 'status' within the union. As a craft union which has opened its membership to unskilled workers in the engineering industry, the union's membership and government conforms to Turner's (1962) definition of an aristocracy, in that a high proportion of union offices are held by members of the 'craft' section (section 1). On the Manchester committee most, if not all, of the members have been section 1 members of the union. This could be anticipated for a number of reasons. The skilled section in Manchester has been nearly twice as large as the unskilled, junior and women's sections combined for most of the post-war period. On this basis alone a proportionate number of elected representatives from section 1 would constitute two-thirds of the committee membership. However, many writers[1] have noted the higher involvement of skilled members in union activities, either because of greater participation in several activities (inside and outside the union) or because of higher stakes in the organisation. Thus on the status dimension, most, though not necessarily all, of the committee members were section 1 members of the union.

A third structural dimension of committee membership is that of plant membership. The studies of Boraston *et al.* (1975) and Edelstein and Warner (1975) indicate that district elections may become dominated by large plants 'with extraordinarily large turnouts, or with members in many of the district's branches' (Edelstein and

Warner, 1975: 179). Unfortunately, the evidence for plant composition of the district committee is lacking, since district records
contain no reference to the plant of origin of the committee members.
There is some evidence, however, that the largest single plant in the
Manchester district, that of Metropolitan Vickers (later AEI), was
always well represented on the committee, both through branch and
shop stewards' elections. It was estimated that during the earlier part
of the study period as many as nine members out of a total of about
thirty-five came from the 'Metrovick' plant, though this later
dropped to only one or two.

The final structural dimension is that of political factions. Again,
evidence of factional memberships of committee members is not
readily available, but in the general terms of a left–right dichotomy,
the evidence of resolutions passed in favour of 'proscribed' organisations suggests a fairly consistent left-wing majority on the committee. In addition, certain key posts such as the District Secretaryship
from 1962 to 1973 and the District Presidency from 1968 to 1970,
have been held by Communist Party members. But equally, it must be
noted that the District President from 1953 to 1959 was Jim Conway
(later General Secretary), a supporter of the Labour Party. In general
though, the tendency was for a left-wing majority, to the extent that
the committee have been described (albeit without justification) as
'all a load of Communists'.[2]

Four structural dimensions of committee membership have been
identified, based on committee experience, union status, plant
membership and factional membership. The lack of records makes it
difficult to determine whether these dimensions are cross-cutting or
correlated, but in general it may be said that committee membership
was predominantly section 1, with a majority of the left-wing faction,
a core of experienced members and for a time a fairly high
representation of the largest plant in the district.

Organisation of committee work in the Manchester districts

The work of each committee is divided between the full committee
and a number of sub-committees. The full committee meets every two
weeks supplemented by special meetings when the need arises. In the
intervening week the sub-committees hold their meetings, usually all
on the same evening.

Up to 1949 the five standing sub-committees were known as the

overtime, piecework, shop stewards, organising, and general purposes sub-committees but, as each sub-committee's work was not
restricted to any particular field, from 1949 onwards they have been
known as sub-committees 1 to 5. These five are supplemented by
special sub-committees which meet less regularly, such as the house
and office, political, motor trade, new machine rates, and library sub-
committees.

Although the meetings of the sub-committees are normally held
very regularly, a certain degree of flexibility remains; occasionally a
sub-committee may not meet or may meet on a different night. As all
of the district committee members engage in sub-committee work the
special sub-committee meetings are always held on a different night
to the standing sub-committeee meetings.

The relationship between the sub-committee meetings and the full
committee meetings is that the chairman of each sub-committee
presents a report to the full committee for adoption. As the district
committee standing orders express it:

> That the procedure in dealing with the business of the
> District Committee shall be that the reports of the sub-
> committee meetings be taken at each District Committee
> immediately after letters from Executive Council,
> expenses and other minor business has been disposed of.
> The chairman of the respective sub-committees to move
> the minutes as a correct record or otherwise. Members of
> the District Committee to be given the opportunity to
> raise questions before they amend or adopt the minutes.[3]

The adoption of the sub-committees' minutes is not a formality, it
being quite common for the minutes to be amended, particularly the
resolutions passed. Rarely are the minutes of all five sub-committees
accepted without amendment, primarily because it is the sub-
committees that perform the major tasks related to trade and
organisation questions in the districts.[4] Communications which have
arrived at the district office from a variety of sources are allocated to
the sub-committees to discuss and for the formulation of resolutions,
occasionally summoning members from the workshops as witnesses.[5]

Though the issues discussed by the sub-committee have remained
similar over the post-war period, the context in which they are raised
has changed. Whereas in the earlier sets of minutes the district
committee was asked to arbitrate or to solve problems, in later

minutes many of the items are notifications of agreements reached in the plant, or are requests for specific pieces of advice. Typical issues raised by conveners or stewards are piecework negotiations, demarcation disputes, overtime and shiftwork questions, and bonus and merit payments. Typical issues raised by branches include the relevant section of membership an individual should join, individual member grievances, as well as the items relating to general 'working conditions' of the type raised by shop stewards. There is now much less actual discussion by the sub-committees, and though the workload appears to have greatly increased the consideration given to each item appears to have reduced proportionately.

This development may be illustrated further by a consideration of what happens to the items which came up for discussion. As noted, the sub-committees pass resolutions at the end of their discussions, and in the minutes of meetings held from 1945 to 1955 a wide variety of resolutions were noted, each specific to the case in hand. For example, many cases would be referred to the Divisional Organiser to follow up, or the sub-committee would recommend the convening of works conferences. Cases which could not be resolved immediately would result in a further sub-committee meeting to which witnesses would be summoned. However, from 1960 through to 1980 it is possible to observe a shift in the locus of decision-taking, in that an increasing proportion of the decisions taken are those of the District Secretary; the sub-committee, having considered the case and the Secretary's response, merely endorses his action. There is clearly a relationship between those two observations: first, that an increasing proportion of items raised by workshops and branches were notifications of agreements and requests for advice, and secondly that the District Secretary had taken over the role of framing and carrying out the appropriate action in reply. Both developments have meant a reduced role for the sub-committees in the formulation of district policy, though the importance of these shifts in decision-taking (particularly that towards the District Secretary) should not be overstated. The sub-committees are under no obligation to endorse the actions of the Secretary, or the full committee to endorse the recommendations of the sub-committee (or the Executive Council to endorse the recommendations of the full committee). The sub-committee may act as a check on the Secretary's activities, for example, by referring issues back to him for further consideration.

Though the sub-committee work is usually the major item for

consideration at a full committee meeting it represents only part of the committee's activity. In addition, there are important items which concern the relationship with the Executive Council and with full-time officers. A typical agenda for a full committee meeting would be:

(1) Minutes of previous full committee metting
(2) Delegates' expenses
(3) Letters from Executive Council
(4) Reports of the sub-committees
(5) Correspondence[6]
(6) District Secretary's report
(7) Divisional Organiser's report

These items in the minutes form the basis of a detailed consideration of the district committee involvement with the Executive Council, workshop organisations, branches and full-time officers. It needs to be re-emphasised, however, that those items in the committee minutes represent only the formal side of the committee's work. Much work is done informally, through meetings and telephone conversations, which either does not appear in the minutes or is formalised later. For example, though there are no formal channels for individual union members to approach the committee, individual contacts in firms provide an additional source of information for the committee which, though impossible to quantify, should not be overlooked.

The Executive Council

The district committee is required to forward the minutes of its meeting to the Executive Council[7] for ratification and this forms the major information flow from the committee to the Council. Most of the correspondence from the Executive Council arises in response to these minutes. Approval is not a formality, the most common grounds for disapproval being that the committee had concerned itself with business which fell outside its scope under Rule 13.[8] Throughout the study period the district committee discussed and passed resolutions on questions as diverse as campaigns sponsored by the *Daily Worker*, Peace Conferences, comments in the mass media, or donations to organisations proscribed by the union. For example, in 1950 the Executive Council disapproved a resolution to send two delegates to an 'All-Lancashire Peace Conference' on the grounds that it was not district committee business. The committee resolved that they could not agree with the Executive Council ruling as 'peace is a subject matter for everybody' (*Minutes*, 15 July 1950). In addition to disapproving these items the Executive Council normally disapproved resolutions arising out of discussions of general union policy (such as national agreements or union government). Heated debate often followed through the correspondence about what is and what is not committee business.

The determination of what can and cannot be discussed by the explicit use of the organisation's written rules is fairly common in the relationship between the district committee and the Executive Council. The rules are not only invoked to define the boundaries of legitimate activity, but also on occasions to stress the legitimacy granted by the rules to particular actions.

Another category of Executive Council correspondence also arises as a response to the minutes but concerns issues of relevance to the district rather than specifically to the committee. Broadly speaking this correspondence falls into four categories:

(1) Correspondence upon disputes in firms, some concerning the engineering industry procedural agreement under which the final stages of negotiation would be conducted by national officers, and some concerning the payment of dispute benefits.[9]

(2) Correspondence upon internal union disputes, or disputes with other unions. The first type of dispute arises between many of the competing polyarchic elements in the union and is often resolved by the Final Appeal Court: the Manchester district has been involved in a number of appeals, both as defendants and appellants. The other type of dispute generally involves accusations that other unions are 'poaching'[10], but such occasions are rare, and inter-union disputes do not appear to have been a major issue in the Manchester district.

(3) Administrative correspondence on such matters as finding branch secretaries, legal claims, acknowledgement of branch resolutions, or appointment of delegates to advisory committees. The range of business is large though the volume is fairly small as the branches handle most of the administrative business.

(4) Trade questions not related to disputes. This is quite a small area of business, mainly concerning questions which affect more than one district, or negotiations which take place at a national level.[11]

A third category of correspondence from the Executive Council is that which is circulated to all district committees. This general correspondence includes circulars on such matters as education facilities, reports from working parties and reminders of union rules, in addition to notification of national agreements. These agreements may affect only a small proportion of members in the district and are dealt with in terms of the minutes either by just 'noting' them or by recommending that the information be passed to the relevant convener or shop stewards. Finally, this category of correspondence also includes requests to all districts to observe the blacking of firms.

Broadly speaking, the correspondence from the Executive Council may be classified into:
(1) information;
(2) clarification of the scope of the district committee's legitimate activities (under rule);
(3) approval or disapproval of business already discussed and resolved upon by the committee.

It appears to be rare for the Executive Council to take the initiative in business which is specific to the district. The Council normally responds to the initiatives of the committee, though it may derive information from branches and full-time officers in addition to that from the committee minutes.

Workshop organisation

Conveners and shop stewards constitute the main formal source of information for the district committee on activity in the district, initiating about 50 per cent of the items raised at committee and sub-committee meetings. The issues raised cover a wide range of trade and organisational questions, but, as noted earlier, the emphasis has changed from requests for intervention to requests for specific advice or notification of agreements. The District Secretary's response normally takes the form of a letter to the convener concerned, though this letter may be preceded by a telephone call if the matter is urgent.

In addition to these formal communications and any informal contacts, shop stewards are required to send quarterly reports to the District Secretary on trade and organisational matters in their plant (for example, the number of engineering workers employed, the number in the union, the number in other unions, and wages and conditions). These reports are then considered by a sub-committee as a means of comparing wages and conditions between plants and as a means of ascertaining whether conditions in any particular plant are satisfactory. However, even these reports are infrequent, often late or missed altogether.

In addition to the responses generated by communications or quarterly reports from the shop stewards the District Secretary writes to inform the stewards of national or district policies affecting their plants.

Though these formal channels of communication exist, they can only play a fairly limited role in control relationships. At several points in their analysis Boraston *et al.* refer to plants 'keeping their affairs to themselves', most notably when they conclude: 'there was little they [the district committee] could do to impose their standards upon powerful workplace organisations which chose to keep their affairs to themselves' (1975: 40). However, Boraston *et al.* do not elaborate on the limitations of the formal communications channels which allow workshop organisations to do this. From the evidence of these channels in the Manchester district it is clear that apart from the sometimes fragmentary quarterly shop stewards' reports there is no formal means whereby the committee can monitor activities in the plants, particularly on a day-to-day basis. Edelstein and Warner (1975: 292) understate the case when they argue 'There is often inadequate contact between the district committee and the shop floor.'

The branches

Information from the branches acts as an important supplement to that derived directly from the workshops. Though the issues raised are the same as those raised by the stewards, the branches tend to be more concerned with individual members rather than groups of workers. Occasionally the issue is a complaint against a workshop organisation, or at least contains the implication that the workshop organisation has not helped the member concerned. The branch would appear to provide an alternative means for individual or group grievances to be brought to the attention of the district committee, other than through conveners or shop stewards. This point is also emphasised by Boraston *et al.*: 'The channel for the dissatisfied steward – or member – is through the branch. About half the letters from branches dealt with industrial matters and most of them drew the attention of the committee to dissatisfaction with the handling of the issue within the plant' (1975: 29). This role for the branch is made possible by the separate bases of branch and workshop organisation. Whereas the shop stewards' organisations are based, naturally enough, on a single plant (or group of plants in a firm) the branches are organised geographically according to members' residence.

This form of organisation is normally held to be a source of weakness for the branches, in that they are divorced from the source of problems that individual branch members may wish to discuss. Similarly, since each branch contains a membership drawn from many firms, an individual member's problem in his plant would raise only limited interest. However, in the control model this separation of organisation is a source of branch strength, since it provides an important check on shop steward autonomy in the workplace; first, by providing the individual member with an avenue of complaint, and secondly, by providing the district committee with information on shop steward activities. Basing the branch on the workplace would tend to produce a single (though not necessarily unified) plant and branch leadership and hence remove this channel from the member and the district committee. Though on the one hand such a move could be interpreted as raising both administrative and representative effectiveness (by providing a more relevant forum for discussion), on the other hand the relative control position of the plant leaderships would be enhanced, strengthening their position in the polyarchy while further weakening that of the rank and file.

Full-time officers

At the district level the two most relevant full-time officers are the District Secretary[12] and the Divisional Organiser.

It has already been noted at several points that the District Secretary's actions are subject to ratification by the sub-committees. In addition, the Secretary presents a report to the full committee, detailing his activities between the meetings. The full committee considers this report, either approving it as a whole or suggesting further consideration on specific items. The number of items in this report varies considerably, partly reflecting the amount of work the Secretary has performed, but also reflecting the time available for the compilation of the report.

According to the rules the District Secretary's main role is administrative. He is required to maintain a list of shop stewards, tabulate wage rates for all plants, keep records of district committee meetings, compile attendance reports on committee members for the branches, audit district funds, keep the district seal for signing documents, and handle the flow of communications into and out of the district office. These activities occupy a large proportion of the Secretary's time (the actual proportion varying from week to week)[13] but are not presented in his report to the committee. This report consists of activities which are performed outside routine administration, activities which may be classified under two headings; first, non-routine administrative tasks, and secondly, negotiation and organisation.

The non-routine administration includes such activities as helping branches in difficulty, meeting with representatives of other organisations, arranging nominations for advisory committees, or representing members at state tribunals. All these aspects of his work the Secretary usually includes in his report.

The more important element of the report, however, concerns his negotiating and organising activities. The only reference that the rules make to negotiation is that the district committee can instruct the District Secretary to enter into negotiations with employers. An examination of the minutes, however, suggests that negotiating and organising takes up a large proportion of the Secretary's time, though this proportion does vary from week to week.

There has been a tendency for the number of items in the Secretary's report to grow, so that although in the 1950s the average number of items was about five, by the 1970s the number was around twenty. In summary, the types of activity which appear in the report are:

(1) visits to branches to sort out administrative difficulties;
(2) representing members at state tribunals;
(3) visits to firms to negotiate over wages and conditions;
(4) visits to firms to meet shop stewards for a discussion of trade problems, organisation or inter-union disputes.

It may be observed that each of these activities involves leaving the district office, and it tends to be this that qualifies an item for inclusion in the report. Not included in the report, therefore, are activities carried out in the district office, even though these activities may involve the resolution of problems arising in firms. These items are generally referred to the sub-committees for endorsement.

The linkages between the district committee and the District Secretary are such that the committee can very largely control the activities of the Secretary. Not only does the committee 'instruct' the Secretary under the rules, but only when the committee has ratified his activities can the Secretary finalise any negotiations. It is important to note, however, that it is the District Secretary who does the negotiating, rather than the committee or sub-committees, and this provides the Secretary with a degree of intimacy with the subject-matter not possessed by the committee. The Secretary thus has access to sources of information about the negotiating process which he can use to present his report in the most favourable light. For example, the committee are not in a good position to question the Secretary's assertion that a particular outcome of negotiations with an employer was the best attainable. Though this places the Secretary at some advantage it does not prevent a dissatisfied committee from instructing the Secretary to reopen negotiations. Though the rules make partial reference to district committees conducting negotiations[14] it would be a mistake to interpret this more widely and to argue, as Edelstein and Warner (1975: 291) for example, that district committees generally negotiate with employers.

The pattern of relationships between the district committee and the District Secretary is repeated in the relationships with the Divisional Organiser (and in Manchester, his assistant). In Manchester the similarity is emphasised not only by the physical proximity of their two offices on the same floor of the building, but also by the Divisional Organiser presenting his report to the committee in person (in the smaller districts of the Division the report is read out 'in absentia').

Rule 16 states that the Divisional Organiser is jointly responsible to the Executive Council and to the district committee of the district in which he is working. Like the District Secretary he is required to present a report of his activities to the committee for endorsement, and may be instructed by the committee to enter into negotiations. During the period when the engineering procedural agreement was in operation the responsibility under the rules for the Divisional Organiser to attend local conferences led to some division of labour between himself and the District Secretary. This procedural agreement between the engineering unions and the Engineering Employers Federation (EEF) required that a grievance within a firm should be the subject of first a works conference, then, if agreement could not be reached, a local conference, and finally, failing agreement at the local level, a national conference. The Divisional Organiser tended to concentrate his activities on firms which were party to the procedural agreement (members of the EEF) whereas the Secretary concentrated on non-federated firms. However, there was a considerable overlap in their activities and it was common for the two officers to visit firms together, either for negotiations with management or for recruitment and organising. Other than for cases in procedure for which he had to be informed, the Divisional Organiser only occasionally derived his choice of activities from the district committee. He appeared to be more independent than the District Secretary, basing his recruiting and negotiating activities more on his own initiative and requests from the workshops. As Boraston *et al.* note, if the Divisional Organiser reported back to the district committee throughout the procedural negotiations at local conferences, these negotiations would have become protracted. The Organiser thus tended to report only concluded negotiations, and if the outcome was acceptable to the Organiser, the firm, and the stewards, it was unlikely that the committee would raise any objections. If the negotiations were concluded with a failure to agree the committee had little option but to pass the issue to the next stage of the procedure.

As with the District Secretary, there would be a tendency for the Divisional Organiser's report to be ratified without too much difficulty, even though the committee had the right, under the rules, to refer the Organiser back to the firm for further negotiations.

Though the two full-time officers are both responsible to the committee, it does not follow that they are always unanimous on the approach to be taken to a given issue. This is illustrated by Turner, when he argues: 'Thus it appeared – at least to an outsider – that at one stage in the Crossley dispute, the District Secretary and District Organiser concerned, both elected, were pulling – from neighbouring rooms in the AEU's Manchester Office – in opposite directions' (1950: 183). In such an instance each officer must try to persuade the committee to support his views. In the above case, for example, the Divisional Organiser persuaded the committee to recommend a return to work, a decision which the District Secretary 'reluctantly' conveyed to the members.

Although the full-time officers have significant areas of autonomy in conducting negotiations, the committee's ability to withhold ratification balances control in the committee's favour, particularly with reference to the District Secretary. The evidence from the Manchester district indicates, furthermore, that such ratification is by no means a formality.

The communications map

Figure 3 represents an elaboration of the communication flows within the union relevant to the district committee.

Issues originate in the workshops and branches, or from other bodies such as other district committees of the union, managements, other unions or fund appeals. Broadly speaking, these issues may be classed as industrial (such as disputes or agreements related to wages, hours, working conditions, redundancy, dismissals or dilution) or organisational (questions of members' status in the union, shop stewards' credentials, union elections, complaints from or about stewards). The District Secretary receives communications from these sources and can take one of four courses of action. First, he can pass the issue to a sub-committee to discuss and resolve upon. Secondly, he can take action himself without leaving the district office (by writing in reply, or by forwarding the communication). Thirdly, he may visit a firm to meet management or stewards, or visit a branch, or a tribunal, and fourthly, a communication may be placed before the full committee for consideration. The full committee considers the action taken, either directly as in the fourth case, or via the sub-committees' and Secretary's reports. Before any of the resolutions carried by the committee are binding upon members in the district they have to be approved by the Executive Council and this is carried out via the committee minutes forwarded by the Secretary. This correspondence from the Executive Council consists largely of responses to these minutes. In addition, it includes notification of national agreements and central conference decisions, and administrative and general circulars.

The Divisional Organiser, acting partly on his own initiative and partly on requests for procedural negotiations, conducts negotiations on a variety of industrial and organisational issues in the district, submitting his actions for approval via his report to the district committee.

Reporting back to the source of the issue occurs through a number of channels, though it should be noted that only when cases are referred to a sub-committee will contact with the source of the issue

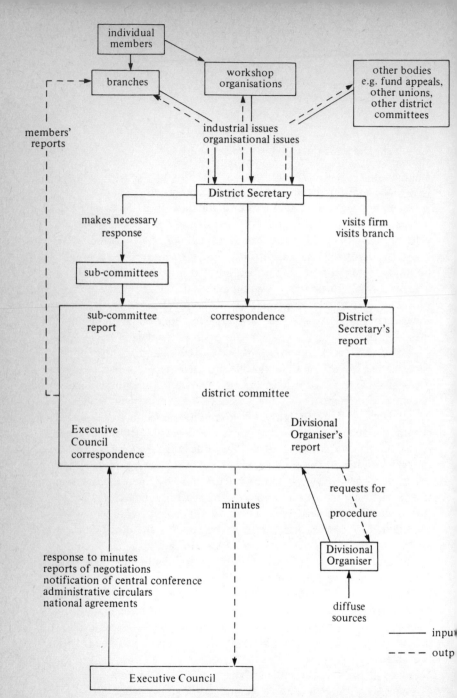

Figure 3 A communications map of district committee activities.

not be immediate (as with visits to firms, or written replies). Problems of reporting back arise when the committee does not endorse the officer's actions, or when the decision is arrived at in committee debate.

Each branch representative may be required to report back to more than one branch, which not only involves a heavy workload for existing representatives but also leaves many branches without representation. It is normal, therefore, for the Secretary to write to those with an interest in a particular decision.

Decisions are also conveyed informally (particularly when urgent), but the channels whereby district committee decisions are conveyed to the membership are very weak, and may be the source of considerable confusion.

Conclusions

Information, exchange and negotiated outcomes

Information has been identified by a number of writers as an important element in a control process. However, it may be observed that information serves a dual purpose in these control relationships, an observation resting on the distinction between the 'quality' of a communications system, and the use of information as a power resource. The former stresses the channels which enable decision-makers to collect information, convey the decision to the area to be controlled, and then monitor the implementation of the decision. Such problems are often treated as communications engineering. Information as a resource stresses the strategic role of information in the exchange process; unless sufficient resources are offered in exchange, information may be deliberately withheld.

The evidence reveals that the formal communication channels between the district committee and the workshops are poor, and this emphasises the importance of the 'voluntary' exchange of information. Without information, the district committee is limited in its decision-taking abilities, a point they recognised when they referred to 'the inability of the district committee to take a decision because of the disregard of Brother Brennan for the district committee' during a dispute with a works convener.[15]

Though the formal channels are poor, evidence from the Manchester district (supported by evidence from Boraston *et al.*'s study) suggests that there are other, informal information channels which can ameliorate, though not entirely compensate for, this inadequacy of the formal channels. The branches, in particular, appear to perform this role, and so too does the practice of summoning witnesses to committee meetings. Communication between the committee and the Executive Council or full-time officers is less problematic. Here there is formal provision for scrutiny on a regular basis, and within the framework of the rules a system of ratification and legitimation that creates ties of dependency beyond those of information exchange.

It is important not to overstate the relevance of information in the production of negotiated outcomes as it is only one of several sources of power based on the ability to offer something in exchange for compliance (for example, expertise). Nevertheless, since the passive membership has been identified as the ultimate source of legitimation, or arbiter of outcomes, the weak link between the membership and the district committee places the workshop organisations at an advantage in any competition between the committee and a workshop organisation.

Legitimation and negotiated outcomes

The rules provide the framework within which competition takes place, though the rules themselves are often the outcome of these competitions. Gouldner (1954) has identified three types of bureaucratic rule: the 'mock bureaucratic' rule, which is only occasionally observed and is broken with impunity, the 'punishment-centred' rule, where sanctions are used for enforcement, and the 'representative' rule, which is seen to be acceptable because it embodies shared meanings, or because it is put forward by people with 'expert' status. Rules in the AUEW(E) tend to be of the 'representative' type, in that compliance is generally perceived to be for the common good. Nevertheless there are limitations on the use of rule alone. Though the rules may establish a framework for behaviour, in practice rules are only part of the control process: behaviour is shaped or controlled without reference to conventional items of rules or commands, through unobtrusive means of control (Perrow, 1973: 291). At the same time, relationships between the committee and the Executive Council are coloured by the wider solidarity principle of the Executive Council. Appeals by the Council to uphold national agreements, and the attempts to limit committee discussions to district questions, are often based on the Executive Council's 'wider responsibilities'. Of the forms of non-contingent legitimacy identified, least emphasis is given to the electoral principle in day-to-day activities. This may be because each of the elements discussed has some claim to electoral legitimacy, and the claims tend to balance out.

Throughout, reference has been made to the manifestations of the various sources of power other than external legitimation and sanctions. In some ways this is misleading, since it is in the nature of these sources that they are usually unarticulated. Control is achieved without explicit reference to the rules, or reference to resources of information and exchange. Though polyarchy has been characterised in terms of competing collectivities, such competition will be predominantly latent rather than manifest, legitimation in particular representing a reason for compliance without overt conflict. Clegg has made a similar point:

> Power relations are only the visible tip of a structure of control, rule and domination which maintain its effectiveness not so much through overt action, as through its ability to appear as the natural convention. It is only when taken-for-grantedness fails, routines lapse, and 'problems' appear that the overt exercise of power is necessary. And this is exerted to reassert control. (1977: 35)

This chapter has emphasised the taken-for-grantedness of the day-to-day control processes within the district committee's areas of activity. As Clegg suggests, it is when this breaks down that competition becomes manifest.

5

The district committee and the Executive Council: a case study in negotiated outcomes

Introduction

When the 'taken-for-grantedness' of decision-making breaks down, competition between collectivities becomes manifest in two forms. In one form the collectivities settle their differences between them, the outcome being determined by each competitor's sources of authority and other forms of power. The outcome produced by this form of competition has been termed a 'negotiated outcome'. The other form of competition, in which the collectivities appeal to agencies external to the competition, produces an 'arbitrated outcome'.

Negotiated outcomes in trade union government rest on the balance of power sources internal to the competitive arena. These, it has been suggested, may be classified as sources of legitimate authority (such as the rule book, the electoral principle and the solidarity principle), and other sources of power (such as sanctions and interdependence). This case study examines the production of a negotiated outcome in the competitive arena which comprises the Manchester district committee and the Executive Council. The substantive issue which created the manifest competition was control over 'dilution' policy in the Manchester district. Following Cole (1973: 48), 'dilution' is generally taken to mean the introduction of less skilled workers to undertake the whole or part of the work previously done by workers of greater skill or experience, often (but not always) accompanied by simplification of machinery or the breaking up of a job into a number of simpler operations.

Post-war dilution in the Manchester district

Disputes with management over job control and internal disputes within the union over local autonomy have been closely related in the history of the AUEW. Both types of dispute have been ascribed by Hinton (1973) to the craftsman's traditional rejection of any form of control over his work, whether from management or from the trade union hierarchy. Though the Manchester district has not figured prominently in the historical struggle against dilution (as compared, for example, with the Clyde) several commentators have noted the post-war resistance to dilution in the district. The Donovan Commission (1968: 69), for example, heard evidence that in Manchester the AEU refused 'to allow such persons [Government Training Centre workers] to be employed as skilled men even if registered as dilutees' according to the national agreement on dilution of labour.

Resistance has been particularly strong to workers from the various post-war government training schemes. On 21 April 1967, for example, Ray Gunter, the Minister of Labour, opening a new Government Training Centre in Manchester, commented: 'The district committee of the AEU, despite the shortage of skilled engineering workers in the area, refuses to accept our engineering trainees' (Hall and Miller, 1971). The national agreement on dilution (Temporary Relaxation of Existing Customs) was introduced in 1939 and simplified in 1941, but instead of being allowed to lapse at the end of the war it continued into peacetime and was amended in 1954. It is to this national agreement that the district committee took exception throughout the post-war period. The Executive Council, on the other hand, as signatories to the agreements, argued that they should be operated. On vocational training, for example, the Executive Council wrote to the district committee in 1953, following the committee's withdrawal of support for the scheme:

> The Vocational Training Scheme Agreement of 1951 was a permissive agreement to provide for the training of certain individuals within the engineering industry, always bearing in mind that such training or employment should not be prejudicial to the employment of our skilled members, and also should have the co-operation of local officials, and was not intended to supersede the Relaxation Agreement.
>
> Within these limits Executive Council feel that the scheme should still continue to operate and that the fullest use should be made of local discussions on this matter where difficulties are encountered.[1]

Though opposition to dilution was strong up to about 1970, it must be recognised that the problem would not be felt equally in all firms in the district. Of the 20 largest engineering firms in the district (that is, employing about a thousand workers or over) only half were engaged upon work which 'dilutee' labour could perform. Dilution is primarily required in those firms with a large machine shop, other firms requiring only very skilled toolroom workers plus a large number of semi-skilled production workers.

District committee/Executive Council relations

Dilution, however, represents only one area in which a divergence of views manifested itself. The historical tensions between local autonomy and centralised control have been examined in some detail in Chapter 3 and the mechanics of the formal relationship between the Committee and the Executive Council have been elaborated in Chapter 4. It is worthwhile emphasising at this point the general lack of agreement which persisted through the post-war period (though, naturally, the intensity or degree of disagreement varied). This may be interpreted as reflecting the fact that some level of disagreement was inevitable or even 'normal' and that it would be unwise to place too much importance upon it. There is evidence, however, that the divergences were not perceived as 'normal' by the participants, but rather were perceived in terms of conflict. Indeed, at a shop stewards' quarterly meeting in 1958 one shop steward used the word 'conflict' to describe the district committee's relationship with the Executive Council.

In Chapter 4 it was noted that the district committee was predominantly left-wing for the whole post-war period. The Executive Council, on the other hand, was predominantly right-wing. It is notable that during those periods when the Executive Councilman for the Manchester district was left-wing (1957/8 and 1964 onwards) there were far fewer recorded disputes.

The disagreements with the Executive Council may be classified under a number of headings:
(1) A branch or a member appeals to the Executive Council over a district committee decision or action. This is quite an important source of disagreement, one or two appeals of this nature occurring every year. When the district committee fines or expels a member, that member has the right to appeal to the Executive

Council. If the Council's ruling is challenged by either the member or the committee the case can be referred to the Final Appeal Court, at which, technically, the Executive Council is the defendant. As might be expected, the disagreements arise when the Council upholds an appeal against the committee.

(2) The use of funds. A number of disagreements have arisen over the committee using funds to contribute to organisations 'proscribed' by the union.

(3) The committee discussing and passing resolutions on matters not covered by Rule 13 (now 12), discussed in more detail in Chapter 4. The dissension largely arises over matters about which the committee might be expected to have some interest, such as circulars from the Executive Council to the branches.

(4) Disputes with particular firms. The Executive Council may disapprove of the committee's actions under this heading for a number of reasons. The most common is that the committee gives its support to a stoppage of work before the Engineering Procedural Agreement has been exhausted. The Executive Council may not only recommend a return to work, but also refuse to make the dispute official (thus precluding the payment of dispute benefit).

(5) General issues of policy. More than any other area of dispute this involves the complex problem of local autonomy. In this instance, autonomy can be seen as ability of the district committee to pursue a policy different from that commended by the Executive Council, not only on dilution, but also such issues as piecework, overtime and redundancy. District opposition to nationally reached agreements occurred in 1956 and 1959 over redundancy policy, and in 1965 over policy on apprentices.

The resolution of these conflicts was achieved without recourse to sanctions, and it is instructive, therefore, to consider the circumstances in which sanctions became necessary in the context of the dilution dispute.

The breakdown of legitimacy

At the National Conference of the union held in June 1951 a new wages claim for the coming round of negotiations was drawn up. In support of this claim the National Committee resolved that: 'This National Committee instruct Executive Council that they shall not agree to any further dilution within the engineering industry until our reasonable demands for a wage increase be granted' (*National Committee Report*, 1951). A number of points need to be made about this resolution. Though the resolution may be interpreted as an expression of labour market strategy, it seems equally reasonable to interpret it as a form of industrial action or policy of non-co-operation which has the advantage of having an economic rationale (the same sort of bargaining strategy as, for example, a temporary overtime ban). In addition, under the 1941 Agreement which amended the conduct of the dilution arrangement the Executive Council would only be involved in dilution at the level of the National Joint Relaxation Committee, after agreement has failed at plant and local levels. Thus for the resolution to prevent dilution it would be necessary for union representatives in the workshops and on local committees to oppose employers' applications for dilution. Equally, it should be noted that the resolution instructs the Executive Council to break a national agreement (though in the context of trade union bargaining, temporary withdrawal from agreed procedures is not in itself uncommon).

The resolution was published as a matter of routine in the July issue of the AEU *Monthly Journal*. The difficulties experienced in Manchester over dilution began that month when the Convener of shop stewards at a firm called Churchill Machine Tools Ltd was approached by the management wanting to upgrade some men to fitters. The stewards considered the National Committee resolution and rejected the management request. When the management made a further approach for the upgrading, the stewards contacted the District Secretary for advice, and were told initially that guidance was being requested from the Executive Council. On being pressed by the stewards for advice, the District Secretary advised that for the time being they should not agree to any dilution.

Later (how much later is not clear from the records) the management told the stewards that they had been advised by the Head Office of the AEU that a circular was being sent to all districts indicating that the resolutions of the National Committee were not to be operated, and management again asked them to agree to dilution. The stewards asked the District Secretary to go to the factory to meet them, and he confirmed that the terms of the Temporary Relaxation Agreement were still in operation as had been indicated in the circular from the Executive Council.

To this point, although the stewards and the district committee would seem to have preferred to implement the National Committee resolution, there were no signs that the issue would develop into one of principle. Following discussions, proposals were agreed for putting to the management as a basis for agreeing to the request for dilution. Though these proposals were put to the management, a meeting of union members in the Fitting Department decided that they were not prepared to accept any dilution. Initially, therefore, the strongest opposition to the dilution came from the members in the workshop.

The management at Churchill's began to put pressure on the Executive Council through the National Employers' Federation. The Executive Council wrote to the district committee and on 6 September 1951 the number one sub-committee carried out an enquiry into the dispute. Letters were read from the Executive Council, the National Employers' Federation and from the Local Employers' Association reporting that the shop stewards had refused to agree to the registration of four men to milling.

After the events of the dispute had been related, the chairman of the shop stewards' committee at Churchill's outlined a number of points to the members of the district sub-committee. First, the shop stewards wanted to have some say in the question of who should be upgraded; they wanted to interview the men and ensure that prospective dilutees were members of the AEU. Secondly, he said, the firm were in the habit of sending for the Convener and asking him to sign the registration forms for dilution without any previous consultation. In concluding his statement to the sub-committee he added that the members in the shop had stated quite categorically that they would not agree to dilution.

Quite clearly, this last point in particular must have placed the sub-committee in a difficult position. On the one hand, the firm was exerting pressure on the Executive Council through the Employers' Federation, yet on the other, there appeared to be a clear refusal on the part of the members to accept dilution. The sub-committee referred the matter to the full district committee (which would have needed to ratify any decision anyway), which advised the stewards at Churchill's not to agree to any further dilution pending advice from the Executive Council, and sent a report of the dispute to the Council.

On 20 September the District Secretary received a letter from the Executive Council outlining the 'official' position that the Temporary

Relaxation Agreement be operated, and criticising the district committee for advising the Churchill stewards otherwise.

The full committee meeting of 27 September considered this letter and a resolution was proposed: 'That this district committee is not satisfied with the reply from Executive Council and request that Bro. R. Openshaw be allowed to attend a meeting of the district committee to hear our views on this matter as we are not prepared to advise our shop stewards of the terms of the letter received from Executive Council.'[2] This resolution did not carry, however, and was succeeded by an amendment that: 'Executive Council be informed we do not agree with the principle of dilution in this district.' This amendment was carried unanimously. The shop stewards' quarterly meeting three days later resolved: 'That this shop stewards' quarterly meeting endorses the attitude of the district committee re the Temporary Relaxation Agreement and its non-operation.' It is at this point that the issue is generalised from dilution at a particular firm to dilution in the district as a whole. Though opposition in principle need not imply that no dilution would be permitted, the implication is clear that the committee and the Secretary would oppose any dilution applications that came within its purview. It must be borne in mind, however, that under the terms of the Agreement, direct control of dilution was not open to the committee. Only through instructions to shop stewards and district officials could a policy of opposition to dilution be pursued. In terms of the effectiveness of opposition to dilution in the district, the support the committee received from the shop stewards' quarterly meeting was important.

Executive Council and the solidarity principle

On 9 October the Executive Council replied to the committee's resolution with a fairly conciliatory letter:

> While the district committee may not agree with the principle of dilution as stated in the resolution ultimately carried by the Manchester district committee until such time as the agreement is terminated it is encumbent upon all districts and members to give effect to the terms of agreement. Executive Council propose to raise with the engineering employers certain aspects of the Relaxation Agreement but at the same time they feel that all points

raised by the Manchester district committee are safeguarded within the terms of the agreement entered into by the Union. Executive Council, therefore, insist on the Agreement being operated and provided that strict observance of the agreement is insisted upon they feel that the apprehensions of your district committee are fully safeguarded.

This appeal to observe agreements reached on behalf of the whole union by national negotiations (and the hint at renegotiations), was not accepted by the district committee. Following the phraseology implied by the National Committee resolution they resolved at their meeting on 11 October: 'That this district committee authorise the District Secretary to inform the Executive Council that the Manchester district committee have only suspended the operation of the Temporary Relaxation Agreement.'

Executive Council and the reaffirmation of legitimacy

The Executive Council then attempted to reaffirm the legitimacy of their action in the eyes of the district committee. On 17 October, they wrote:

Executive Council note the reasons which are apparently influencing the district committee in their attitudes and decisions. It is apparent that your district committee do not as yet clearly understand the factual position in connection with any or all resolutions carried by the National Committee. In the first place it must be clearly understood that National Committee resolutions are instructions to the Executive Council who decide when and how these resolutions are to be operated, and there is no evidence that we know of that justifies your committee in even assuming that this particular resolution will not be given effect at the appropriate time and in a way which in the opinion of Executive Council will obtain the best results for the members. It is quite obvious, if you examine the large number of resolutions adopted by the National Committee, that very often contributions to the discussion which help to guide the members of the National Committee in adopting the resolution have to be taken into account by the Executive Council.

This attempt to restore legitimacy had no more effect than the appeal to observe national agreements. It became clear to the Executive Council that there was no longer any basis in legitimate authority to which it could appeal in order to get the district committee to follow its instructions. The district committee had denied that the Executive Council could legitimately refuse to operate the National Committee minutes and had refused to implement a nationally agreed procedure.

Application of sanctions

On 23 October the Executive Council sent a further letter to the District Secretary which was discussed at a special meeting of the district committee on 1 November. At the request of the District Secretary the Chairman and Secretary of the Churchill shop stewards' committee were also present. The letter which was read to the meeting emphasised again that shop stewards and district committees were bound to give effect to agreements entered into by the union. It pointed out that the district committees had no authority to suspend any agreement, and that 'the Executive Council could no longer tolerate a flouting or evasion of their instructions'. The letter continued:

> This letter must be placed before the district committee, and Executive Council desire to be informed of the members of the district committee who either abstain from voting or voting against giving effect to Executive Council instructions, and in conformity with Rule 22 Clause 1 intimate their intentions to proceed against such members under the said Rule and Clause, lines 10–13 – 'or refuse to comply with the order or decision of any committee, council or conference having jurisdiction over such member under these rules' and lines 25–28 – 'or who being an officer shall have refused to perform their duties imposed upon him by these rules or any of them, may be expelled by his Branch, with the approval of the Executive Council, or he may be expelled or otherwise dealt with by the Executive Council'. Executive Council desire the information by 5 November 1951.

What this quotation from the rules does not convey very clearly is that 'may be expelled or otherwise dealt with' applied not only to the officer of line 25 but to the whole of Clause 1. Thus all of the members of the district committee were threatened with disciplinary action, the most extreme form of which would have been expulsion from the union. (In the 1980 *Rule Book*, the phrase 'or otherwise dealt with' is amended to read 'or suspended from office or fined by the Executive Council'. Though not spelt out in the Rules of 1951 these would appear to be the sanctions other than expulsion available to the Executive Council.)

The minutes of the meeting note that the discussion following the reading of the letter was lengthy and heated. The shop stewards' chairman stated that the management were still unwilling to meet shop stewards on the dilution question. He said that the management were not prepared to specify their requirements; they wanted assurances that the terms of the Temporary Relaxation Agreement would be operated and that as and when they wanted dilution in the factory it would be granted. Only then would they be prepared to discuss the conditions under which the upgraded men could work.

Concern was expressed at the meeting that it appeared to be the employers rather than the shop stewards who were trying to breach the Agreement. In the event of shop stewards not approving an application for dilution the case should have been referred to the Local Relaxation Committee. The employers' insistence on imposing dilution unilaterally was a breach of the Agreement, and the Executive Council was criticised by the meeting for not supporting the district committee on this point.

The minutes record that the majority of the committee were not only very critical of the decisions which the Executive Council had taken, but also of the means whereby they were being enforced. But eventually, on the advice of the District Secretary, the following resolutions were adopted:

1. That this district committee accept the decision of Executive Council on this matter under protest.
2. That this district committee express concern at the terms of the Temporary Relaxation Codified Agreement.
3. That the Conveners in the district be advised of the

decision of the district committee on the letter received from Executive Council.

4. That this district committee disapprove of the terms of the letter dated 23 October, and ask under what Rule does Executive Council have the power to state that they are the body who shall decide how and when National Committee decisions are operated.

5. That we ask for the voting of Executive Council members on this question which resulted in the letter of 23 October being sent.

A further resolution, signed by 277 members at Churchill's was forwarded: 'We the undersigned members of the AEU employed at Churchill Machine Tools request the district committee to press Executive Council to recall the 1951 National Committee and explain their reasons for the non-implementation of the 1951 National Committee Resolution Number 54.'

It is clear from these resolutions that this issue had been resolved in favour of the Executive Council. In the Council reply to the district committee no more was said on dilution except to repeat that they intended to raise the Agreement with the Employers' National Federation. The Council vote on the decision to send the letter had been unanimous, they reported. The Council did make another attempt to reassert their authority on the 'resolution problem':

> Executive Council point out that in the absence of any specified date being laid down by National Committee for the operation or application of resolutions it must be left to Executive Council as the governing body of the union to decide in accordance with the circumstances at what time it is appropriate to operate certain resolutions . . . It cannot be the prerogative of a district committee to select one resolution and to decide to operate such . . . and it will be for the National Committee, not any district committee, to pass judgement on Executive Council in respect to their actions upon decisions passed by that body.

As far as the evidence of the minutes reveals, this marked the conclusion of this particular incident. It is perhaps worth re-emphasising that the committee did not pursue the case to arbitration by either the Final Appeal Court (there being no ground, under rule, on which the case could have been fought) or the rank and file in the district.

Underlying the rationale of this course of action is the pervasiveness of the union's electoral system and the existence of factions. As has been emphasised, the AUEW(E) is characterised by both a vigorous electoral system and factional groupings. That the issue was not thrown open to membership arbitration may be ascribed in part to the risk of that arbitration producing a right-wing majority on the district committee.

In this sense, it may be argued that the passive membership exercised a latent arbitral role even though the issue was not referred to them. However, since the issue was resolved without manifest arbitration, the term 'negotiated outcome' remains appropriate.

In addition, committee members stressed in interview that they valued their position on the committee as a participation in union activities; removal from the committee represented an important sanction.

The post-sanctions phase

It has been noted that agreement between the district committee and the Executive Council was low throughout the post-war period. The outcome in favour of the Executive Council in 1951 did not reduce the general level of dissension. On dilution, however, the next few years subsequent to 1951 show a marked change in committee decisions. In May 1952, less than six months after the Churchill dispute, a problem arose in the Tank Shop at Ferranti's. The Convener informed the no. 1 sub-committee that the shop stewards were not prepared to operate the Relaxation Agreement because the introduction of dilutees had affected skilled earnings (through slower working and hence a lower contribution to a Pool Bonus Scheme). The sub-committee resolved: 'That we cannot agree to dilution at Ferranti's if it means our members will lose financially', and also: 'That we instruct the convener to open negotiations with management to ensure that our members do not lose financially.'

By referring the matter back to the firm the sub-committee was able to avoid having to make a decision. They were able to do this again in July of that year when a dispute arose in the Transformer Machine Shop at Ferranti's. The members in the shop felt that if they were accepted the dilutees would be given the 'large-batch', easier jobs, while the earnings of the skilled men would be reduced because they would have to do the jobs involving frequent setting up. The members had decided to refuse the application and also to refuse co-operation if dilutees were introduced. The sub-committee resolved that: 'In view of the fact that there are no real grounds for refusing dilution we advise our members to comply with the terms of the Temporary Relaxation Agreement.' But this resolution was qualified with another: 'That the district committee advise the Engineering Employers' Association that our members are reluctant to co-operate; therefore, the management must make themselves responsible for the supervision required.'

Again, the sub-committee compromised but nevertheless advised that the Agreement be operated. For the next few years the pattern of dilution cases was the same. Under the Relaxation Agreement the committee could only become involved indirectly if the stewards in a firm objected to a dilution application, and even then they could only 'instruct' or advise shop stewards or the representatives on the Local Relaxation Committee (usually the Divisional Organiser). The stewards' complaints were usually over earnings, and in each case the committee either recommended a rejection of dilution until the earnings issue had been settled or recommended that dilution be accepted and earnings negotiations take place. A typical dilution resolution was the one in July 1952 over dilution at Churchill's:

> That in view of the fact that there are a number of anomalies affecting the earnings of our skilled members arising from the introduction of dilutees, we instruct our shop stewards to open negotiations with management with a view to removing these anomalies, as until they are resolved we are not prepared to advise our shop stewards to agree to the present application.

During this period the 1954 Codified Agreement replaced the 1941 Agreement, and the minutes record only a noting of the new clauses, even though the new agreement created a new class of jobs; that is, those which were registered under the existing agreement. On these jobs additional dilutees could be introduced with only prior consultation with the shop stewards. Under the earlier agreement the stewards at least had the right to refer cases to a Local Joint Relaxation Committee. The district policy, as far as one can be identified, appeared to be that the Relaxation Agreement should be operated.

The re-emergence of district legitimacy: the Platt's closure, 1956

In 1956 the proposed closure of Platt's (Barton) Ltd, manufacturers of textile machinery, created the prospect of 2,000 jobs being lost in the Manchester district. Of these a good proportion would have been those of skilled workers and so, on 10 October, the no. 5 sub-committee met to consider the question of dilution in the district. They resolved:

> That we agree to defer any further dilution until all the skilled men at Platt's are absorbed elsewhere. The question of agreeing to further dilution be considered again when it is known that the skilled men in each particular trade have been absorbed. At this stage, consideration be given to dilutees taking similar jobs in other factories where they should be re-registered.

As has been shown before, such a blanket ban on dilution is contrary to the Agreement, which insists that each application must be considered, and, if necessary, pursued through the Relaxation Procedure. On 30 October the no. 1 sub-committee considered a number of letters from conveners in the district advising that they had received upgrading applications from their management. As a number of stewards were being pressed by their managements for a decision, the District Secretary suggested to the sub-committee that a firm decision was required. The sub-committee agreed to the request at three firms 'in view of special circumstances' but passed a more general resolution: 'That our shop stewards be advised that we are not prepared to grant permission until fully skilled men affected by the proposed closure of Platt's are absorbed.'

Just under a month later the Local Relaxation Committee considered the closure of Platt's as well as a 20 per cent redundancy at a firm in the neighbouring Ashton district. The trade union representatives refused to permit any further dilution until a more stable labour position was established, so the employers referred the matter to the National Relaxation Committee. The district committee (in a resolution to the Divisional Organiser's report) endorsed the stance of the representatives at the Local Committee. The Employers' reference to the National Relaxation Committee was held on 5 December (the District Secretary represented the district committee), and after discussion the matter was referred back for discussion locally 'in the light of existing circumstances'. At the subsequent Local Committee meeting in January 1957 the trade union representatives were not prepared to change their minds and decided that 'dilution will continue to be resisted throughout the *division* whilst the present conditions remain' (my emphasis).

The district committee was thus able to derive legitimacy for its opposition to dilution from a number of sources. First, the closure of Platt's meant not only that there existed unemployed skilled members whose job rights they needed to protect but also that the Agreement was being operated in principle (the employers could not prove that no skilled labour was available). Secondly, to some extent the Agreement had been operated, since the matter was referred to the National Relaxation Committee which, unable to reach a decision, had referred it back. Thirdly, the ban stemmed not from the Manchester district alone but also the other districts in Division 11 (Stockport, Ashton, Newton and Warrington) covered by the Local Relaxation Committee. The policy was only outside the Agreement in so far as blanket opposition to dilution was outside the Agreement.

The Executive Council wrote to the district committee insisting that the Agreement be operated. After a discussion of this letter and the correspondence related to the Employers' reference to the Local Committee the no. 4 sub-committee resolved: 'That we instruct all shop stewards to forward all applications for dilution to the district committee for agreement or otherwise.' When the full committee considered the matter a week later the District Secretary pointed out that he was required to write to the Executive Council on the subject and felt that a firm opinion should be expressed by the committee. The previous decision to ban dilution was reaffirmed.

A further exchange of letters between the Executive Council and the committee then followed, the Executive Council insisting that the Agreement be operated, the committee replying 'that we are operating the spirit and intention of the Agreement'.

The Employers again referred the matter to the National Relaxation Committee at which one strand of the legitimacy of district committee opposition was removed. It was decided that: 'In view of statements made by the Employers as contained in the short-hand notes, the Union representatives agreed that the Relaxation Agreement be implemented.'

The district committee still attempted to retain some control over dilution, and on 26 April 1957 the Executive Council wrote to report that the Employers were considering a referral of the dilution issue to the Industrial Disputes Tribunal. Though the committee relaxed its ban during June and July the Employers were concerned to remove any control over dilution from the district committee. In September the Manchester Engineering Employers' Association referred the case to the Industrial Disputes Tribunal. The Ministry of Labour suggested a meeting of the parties before the hearing of the Tribunal, to which the Divisional Organiser agreed, though he also requested specific details of the Employers' allegations that the Agreement was not being operated. The Organiser presented his report of this procedure to the district committee, and at the same meeting the committee agreed to an application for dilution, 'bearing in mind the report of the Divisional Organiser'.

At the pre-tribunal meeting the Employers insisted on proceeding to arbitration on all firms where agreement on dilution could not be reached, though the trade union view was that where sufficient reason was given for refusing the applications this could not constitute a dispute. The reference to the Tribunal was withdrawn and a meeting of the National Relaxation Committee arranged. At this national meeting it was agreed that the matter should be referred back for decision locally. The district committee, considering the meetings which had taken place, resolved: 'That this district committee endorse the action of the Divisional Organiser in advising the Engineering Employers' Association that there will be no further dilution whilst the present position obtains.'

The evidence suggests, however, that in spite of this resolution there do not appear to have been great difficulties over dilution after this date. The issue appeared occasionally in the minutes but usually as a formality or where the shop stewards wanted to discuss some related question. On the few occasions when this resulted in a refusal of the applications the employers usually protested to the Executive Council who wrote to the district committee insisting that the Agreement be operated. There is no evidence that these cases raised any of the problems that occurred in 1951 and 1956. By the 1970s the attitude towards dilution was changing. Rapidly changing skill requirements and the development of training and retraining began to make dilution less of an issue. Symptomatic of this shift of values was the appointment of Hugh Scanlon as Chairman of the Engineering Industry Training Board in the spring of 1975.

Concluding comments

The question that must be asked is why the district committee's statements on banning dilution did not arouse the same degree of Executive Council hostility in 1956 as in 1951. Certainly, the Executive Council wrote many times in 1956/7 insisting that the district committee operate the Agreement, but they did not resort to sanctions. That they did not do so may be accounted for in a number of ways. First, although the district committee stated that dilution was banned there is evidence that the ban was operated reasonably flexibly. Even immediately after the resolution banning dilution in September 1957 there is little evidence of dilution problems occurring. It is possible to argue, therefore, that the district committee, mindful of the events of 1951, were not prepared to push opposition to dilution to that level where the Executive Council would be impelled to take more severe action. Secondly, in 1956 the district committee could legitimise their actions on the ground that there were skilled workers unemployed, that the procedural agreement was being partially implemented, and that all the other districts in the division were involved in the ban. Thirdly, the position taken by the district committee on Resolution 54 in 1951 may be interpreted as a challenge to the policy-making freedom of the Executive Council, not in the single area of dilution policy but on the whole question of the implementation of National Committee resolutions. The degree of Executive Council control over policy-making has been a contentious issue in union affairs throughout its history. The problems of 1951 may thus be interpreted as a dispute over legitimacy in general whereas in 1956 general principles were not at stake.

A fourth reason may be that during the dispute in 1957 the Executive Councilman dealing with Manchester affairs was Les Ambrose, a left-winger, which may have raised the general level of agreement between the parties.

Legitimacy is important in any consideration of the threat of sanctions and its effectiveness. Though it was a breakdown of legitimacy which in part made the threat of sanctions necessary, the imposition of sanctions was perceived as legitimate by the district committee; there were no references, in the discussion at the relevant committee meeting, to the Executive Council 'having no right' to impose the sanctions. This regard for the legitimacy derived from the Rule Book has been noted in Chapter 3. And as Fletcher (undated: 4) puts it: 'Democracy therefore entails the acceptance of the "rule of law" within the union and, as a result, a meticulous and legalistic attitude towards the rule book.'

The outcome produced in this competition may justifiably be termed 'negotiated' since although the district committee were pressed by shop stewards, and the Executive Council were pressed by the employers, neither party appealed to outside arbiters in the dispute. The Executive Council used sanctions granted to it by the Rule Book and the district committee complied because of dependence on Committee membership. If it were argued that the district committee members might have been expelled from the union and thus possibly put out of work, the basis of dependence would be altogether different. It seems unlikely, however, that the Executive Council would have gone this far with their sanctions. Dissolving the committee would have been sufficient to achieve their aim of control over the dilution issue in the district; expulsion might have escalated the dispute within the district, or even generalised it within the union as a whole.

6

The district committee and a workshop organisation: a case study in arbitrated outcomes

Introduction

Arbitrated outcomes have been described as those outcomes of a competition which are reached by appeal to an agency (arbitrator) external to that competition. In Chapter 2, the employers and the passive membership were identified as significant sources of legitimation for rival collectivities in a trade union and it is this ability which makes it possible for them to arbitrate an inter-collectivity competition.

This chapter examines the process of outcome arbitration in a competition between the Manchester district committee and the shop stewards' organisation in the largest engineering firm in the Manchester district. As has been argued earlier, such relations involve a process of 'negotiation of order'. Stable working relations evolve out of the expectations and obligations that develop. Periodically, however, these understandings can break down and the problem of power inherent in the relationship may generate overt conflict.

The firm in which this case study is located produces heavy electrical engineering products in two factories in the Manchester district, the larger built in Trafford Park before the First World War and the other a transformer factory built in Wythenshawe in 1955. Founded at the turn of the century by the Westinghouse Corporation in America it came under British ownership during the First World War as Metropolitan-Vickers Ltd, reverted to part American ownership again in 1928 (when it became part of Associated Electrical Industries) and reverted back to British ownership in 1953. As part of the search for a corporate identity the Metropolitan-Vickers title was dropped in 1960 in favour of AEI (Manchester) Ltd.

Takeover by the General Electric Company in 1967 was followed quickly by merger with English Electric in 1968. The rationalisation which followed these changes accelerated the reductions in manpower which AEI had been implementing during the 1960s, so that an estimated work-force of 15,000 manual workers at Trafford Park just after the Second World War, was reduced to less than 5,000 in 1970,[1] and about 3,500 by 1980.

The plant organisation contained several features likely to make control by the district committee more difficult. Over twenty trade unions were represented on the twenty-strong workers' side of a works committee (this committee, with representatives both of trade unions and management was set up in 1917), density of union membership was high, and a large number of issues (particularly concerning piecework) were traditionally dealt with in the workplace, allowing trade union experience to develop. However, the plant organisation was not always unified, one area of friction being between some ETU and AEU stewards.

This chapter examines three occasions of overt conflict between the district committee and some of the AEU stewards on the workers' side of the works committee (most notably, the AEU Convener of Shop Stewards, Bert Brennan). Two of these occasions centred around strike calls and the third around the redundancy problem of the late 1960s.

Before examining these incidents in detail it is worth re-emphasising some general points about the relationships between shop steward organisations and trade union hierarchies.

Sources of workshop organisation independence

Although Rule 12 of the union Rule Book provides for district committee control in relationships with workshop organisations, the extent to which a district committee can exercise this control is severely limited in practice by a number of constraints.

The first of these is information flow. The information which the district committee receives from workshop organisations is extremely variable in quantity and quality. Shop stewards' quarterly reports are a formal channel whereby information about density of union membership and wage rates in force are conveyed to the District Secretary and hence to the committee. However, even when these are fully and promptly returned they cannot convey information about issues which arise on a day-to-day basis such as disputes. As an alternative to information coming from the shop stewards the committee can and does receive communications from individual members, either directly or indirectly via a branch, and from managements.

However, individual members who do not attend branch meetings (and, therefore, do not hear the committee representative's report) are unlikely to be in a position to know what is district committee policy. Similarly, managements will not usually be aware of district committee policy and will only complain to the District Secretary or the Employers' Association if they feel that national agreements are being infringed contrary to their (the employer's) interests. Thus the committee may find it difficult to ascertain whether or not its decisions are being complied with in the workplace.

The second of these constraints is the role of shop stewards in the maintenance of the organisation. Several writers have noted that shop stewards play an important part in the recruitment of members and the collection of union dues. Goodman and Whittingham (1973) have argued that the competition between unions for members has limited the extent to which sanctions can be applied to shop stewards. Many union officials, they suggest, consider that expulsion not only creates martyrs and hostility to the union but also removes offenders from the union's influence while not preventing them from influencing union members. In the AUEW the rules provide that other than under check-off agreements contributions must be paid at branch meetings and therefore imply that collection by stewards at the place of work is contrary to rule (Rule 3, Clause 11). However, according to McCarthy (1966) all the AEU stewards in the Royal Commission's study collected contributions each week, and in the Clegg, Killick and Adams (1961) survey it was found that 68 per cent of AEU shop stewards collected contributions. The Clegg *et al.* survey shows that shop stewards do almost as much collecting in a union which makes no provision for it, and in which the practice appears to be contrary to rule, as in unions whose rules prescribe for the appointment and payment of collecting stewards. However else, asks McCarthy, could the Engineers collect contributions in a large factory in which they organise hundreds or even thousands of members who certainly could not be persuaded to attend branch meetings regularly? The introduction of 'check-off' schemes would weaken McCarthy's argument but in their absence the shop steward plays a major role. The part played by shop stewards in carrying out essential union functions means that full-time officers or lay committees such as the district committee must be very careful to give the impression that the shop steward's work is appreciated and to give the shop stewards support whenever possible. McCarthy suggests that only in extreme cases, where shop stewards have systemically defied instructions or have led open revolts against accepted union policies, is it possible to withdraw credentials or expel dissident members without giving rise to a widespread conviction that they have been unfairly treated or punished for defending the workers' interests.

The third constraint lies in the relationships between shop stewards and work groups. Sanctions are difficult to apply because shop stewards have a closer relationship with the members than the full-time officers or lay committees. Because of the close knowledge that the shop steward has of plant affairs and because he is directly elected by the work group he represents it may be argued that the authority of shop stewards is perceived by the members as being more legitimate than those of 'outsiders'. As Fox notes:

> It must suffice to say that in some situations the individual may come to feel that his only real refuge is his immediate work group. Loyalty to that group and its leader may then rank as a prior obligation. Especially is this likely to be the case where the work group has proved the most effective instrumental level through which the individual goals are pursued. If, at the same time, the group members find themselves in normative conflict not only with management but also with some higher-level collectivity of their union, and unable therefore to legitimize the policies of either, the strength of their identification with the work group as their only source of legitimate leadership is likely to be very great. (1971: 112)

Though this is probably true it should be borne in mind that the relationships between shop stewards and work groups are very complex, as indicated by Batstone *et al.*'s study (1977) of shop stewards in the motor industry. Not only is the notion of a work group itself vague, but also different groups will interpret the role of stewards differently, as too will different stewards. Batstone *et al.* observed that some stewards 'lead' member opinion amongst their members while others 'follow' what they believe opinion to be. Goodman and Whittingham have drawn attention to the divergences which may arise between shop stewards and work groups, particularly when stewards' associations develop bureaucratic tendencies and become dissociated from the work groups they represent. Since the relationships between shop stewards and work groups can vary quite considerably, so too will the extent to which members orient themselves to the plant organisation as a collectivity. It is where this orientation is strong that restraints are imposed upon the ability of full-time officials and lay committees to apply sanctions against members of the plant organisation.

The fourth problem is that of multi-unionism. The tendency of shop stewards' associations to develop bureaucratic tendencies may produce a rift between stewards and workplace members. These associations are often composed of a number of unions and pose difficulties of control not only for members but also for higher levels in the collectivities. McCarthy (1966) notes that where multi-unionism exists individual union control becomes difficult. The Trades Union Congress Annual Report of 1960 stated that 'cases of muddle, duplication and even conflict have arisen through these bodies acting as though they were independent of union obligations' (TUC 1960: 129). Problems of control arise particularly when one union is attempting to impose a policy on the workshops whereas the other unions are not. With reference to an overtime agreement in the 'Leachester' district Boraston *et al.* found that because production workers were divided between unions, and the other unions had little regard for the agreement, it was impossible to control the overtime worked by AEU production workers (1975: 35).

Fifth and lastly, constraints are created by the existence of other sources of workshop organisation independence. To some extent the factors already considered, by making plant organisations less liable to sanctions, may be sources of independence from control by full-time officials and the district committee. There are, however, a number of other factors which allow workshop organisations to build up their strength within a plant and become less dependent on union assistance. McCarthy (1966) identifies the state of the labour market, the socio-technical system of the plant, the level of decision-taking, the wage structure, the scope of agreements, and employer, union and work group attitudes as the main determinants of the behaviour and influence of shop stewards. Goodman and Whittingham see the influence of shop stewards in a plant as being much more a function of trade union organisation. In particular they identify multi-unionism, branch apathy, vague rule books, the paucity of full-time officials, and the role of shop stewards as work group leaders, as contributing to what they call 'shop steward power'; though in addition they also mention loose industry bargaining and the willingness of management to concede to force. It must be expected that there will be differences in shop steward organisation and role both according to the industry and to the unions involved.

Boraston *et al.* (1975) suggest that from the evidence of their studies many of the factors considered above are not as generally important as has been thought. For example, it does not appear to have made much difference to workshop independence whether branches are organised geographically (when apathy is said to be highest) or organised on the basis of workplace. Similarly they found that the availability of full-time officers has some effect on workplace independence, but this effect is limited, and their case studies produced no instances of a wide scope for bargaining encouraging independence (1975: 167 and 180). The variable that they found to be of greatest importance was the size of the workplace organisation, since the larger this is, the greater the resources at its disposal and the more independent its behaviour. In addition to the size factor they argue that resources will be larger the greater is the unity within a workplace organisation, the trade union experience of its members and their status as employees.

In view of these difficulties in achieving control over workshop organisations by the union outside the plant, and in particular in applying sanctions, it is possible to agree with Goodman and Whittingham's argument that unions have little effective redress against stewards that exceed their authority and assume the power to extend their role (1973: 178).

The negotiation of areas of legitimate decision-making

In most organisations areas of autonomy in the making of certain decisions become defined through some process of informal negoti-ation. The orderly day-to-day working relationships which are the outcome of these negotiations emerge only slowly and may be fragile at best. In this case study two such processes are involved. First, there is the historical development, over the period of the study, of the relationships between the district committee and the workshop organisation. Secondly, there is the equally important way in which the workshop organisation, and the Convener in particular, developed their relationships with the management in the plant.

The negotiations over autonomy and legitimacy between the workshop organisation and the district committee occur at the outset of this case study in 1946. Unusually for such negotiations they took an overt form, highlighting the lack of clarity in the formal position of shop stewards and conveners with reference to their unions outside the plant. It is also worth noting at this point that it was not until 1968, twenty-two years later, that the outcome of those negotiations was referred to by the Convener as a source of legitimation for his actions.

The problem arose with a dispute during the Second World War between the shop stewards of the AEU and those of the ETU on the works committee, concerning the type of procedure to be followed in the factory. The ETU claimed an arrangement had been reached with management allowing the ETU chief shop steward to approach the superintendents or higher management without the consent of the works committee man for the area concerned. An AEU member objected to this with the result that the works committee (which at that time had a majority of AEU members) repudiated the agreement, on the grounds that they could not agree to one union being in a favoured position. Chris Blackwell, the ETU chief steward, had brought the question up on the Area Committee of the ETU and they had endorsed the procedural agreement he had reached with management.

At a joint meeting of representatives of the ETU and AEU, held on 29 January 1946, Hugh Scanlon, the AEU Convener of shop stewards, put forward the opinion that a question of principle was involved – should the sole responsibility for negotiations rest with the works committee or should any separate union be entitled to carry on negotiations without the knowledge of the works committee? He suggested that the procedure which the ETU were attempting to establish was cutting out entirely the works committee procedure and would mean each separate union conducted its own negotiations.

It can be seen that Hugh Scanlon's question of principle was anything but an 'either/or' problem. He posed the two possibilities as being 'sole responsibility' with the works committee, or 'without the knowledge of' the works committee. Clearly, these are rather extreme alternatives but nevertheless the joint meeting resolved 'That the Works Committee shall be solely responsible for negotiations within the firm.' Of course this resolution established an awkward precedent with regard to the position of full-time officers and the district committee. The Executive Council of the AEU in a letter to the district committee (dated 25 February 1947) noted this resolution but asked for its terms to be made clear with respect to the position of full-time officers. There appears to be no evidence of whether this was ever done, but the resolution was never amended.

It should be noted that the reasons for this dispute were more than just inter-union rivalry. By putting responsibility for negotiations onto the works committee the resolution gave added importance to the role of the AEU Convener, a post held at this time by Hugh Scanlon, then a member of the Communist Party and a notable local militant. Similarly, the repudiation of the agreement achieved by the ETU reduced the role of the ETU chief steward, Chris Blackwell, a prominent local Catholic and Labour Party supporter. Not only were there factional problems between the two unions but also within them, particularly within the ETU. In late 1948, Chris Blackwell had his credentials withdrawn by the ETU district committee after a minor shop dispute in which a Communist shop steward of the same union was involved. As Turner says: 'Many of the inter-union and politico-religious conflicts which culminated in the Blackwell affair of 1948 had centred in this body (the Works Committee at Metropolitan-Vickers)' (1950: 208). The AEU district committee, under whose auspices the joint meeting had been held, was probably fairly satisfied with the outcome, as Hugh Scanlon, a district committee member himself, appeared to have a good relationship with the committee and kept them fully informed of developments within the plant. In 1947, however, he was elected to the post of Divisional Organiser and his place as AEU Convener was taken by Bert Brennan who had been his deputy.

The dispute: phase I

It was not until late 1951 that the first of the major difficulties arose between the district committee and the works committee. The issue was the dismissal of Benny Rothman, an AEU shop steward and works committee man (though not on the district committee). Benny Rothman was a militant shop steward who spoke of himself as 'a thorn in the side of the management', and it was believed by the district committee that his dismissal was directly related to his trade union activities. At a full district committee meeting on 22 November 1951 standing orders were suspended to hear representatives from Metropolitan-Vickers who had stopped work because of his dismissal.

The dispute arose on 20 November 1951 when a welder was given a job to do without a fitter, previous practice in the works being that the fitter worked in conjunction with the welder. The welder was instructed to proceed with the job under threat of dismissal. Three leading stewards all viewed the work concerned and agreed that it was a fitter and welder's job whereupon the men in the department stopped work. Benny Rothman decided to call a meeting in his own department, at which it was decided to support the action of the men in the department where the dispute had arisen. He was dismissed for 'participating in a stoppage', and as a result the men in the West Works stopped work. At a meeting following the stoppage they decided that they were not prepared to resume work until Rothman was reinstated.

Hugh Scanlon (now Divisional Organiser) and the District Secretary, who were present at the factory for a works conference on other matters, heard of the dispute and asked Bert Brennan, the Convener, to arrange an informal meeting with the Assistant Works Manager, Mr Main. Through the shop stewards the men were asked to resume work to allow these informal discussions to take place, and this they did. However, at this informal meeting between the Divisional Organiser, the District Secretary and the management, the management refused to expand on the statement that Benny Rothman was dismissed for participating in a stoppage, though Mr Main argued, so the district committee was told, 'This is a question for the management to decide, I am running this factory and I am going to have discipline.'

When the results of this meeting became known, the men in the West Works again stopped work, and this was how the situation stood when the district committee met on 22 November 1951. Considerable discussion took place and the following resolution was moved and seconded:

> That this district committee is of the opinion that the week's notice given to Brother Rothman is a straightforward case of victimisation and constitutes a threat to the shop stewards in the area.

It further declares its appreciation of the action taken by the workers in the West Works and hereby decides to call a meeting of all members at Metropolitan-Vickers on Friday noon 23 November 1951 to call support of the action taken by the members in the West Works.

An amendment was then put that the second part of the resolution should be deleted and 'that a meeting of workers be called by the Works Committee on this issue' be inserted. The voting on the amendment was 14–14 and the President ruled that the resolution was not carried. A further amendment was put that the second part of the resolution should read: 'It further declares its appreciation of the action taken by the workers of the West Works and instructs the AEU Convener to call a meeting of our members on Friday 23 November 1951 on this issue.' The second amendment was carried 13 votes to 12, and the whole resolution was carried 19 to 4.

From the narrowness in the voting margins on the second part of the resolution it seems clear that there was a large split of opinion within the district committee, the main area of difference being whether or not to try to spread the stoppage from the West Works to other parts of the Metropolitan-Vickers factory. Though he was a district committee member, Bert Brennan was not present at this meeting. The day following the meeting the District Secretary rang Brennan to inform him of the district committee's resolution. The content of their phone call become a source of some confusion, Bert Brennan claiming initially (in a report submitted through the Divisional Organiser) that the District Secretary had instructed him to call a meeting to gain support. At a later sub-committee meeting after the strike Bert Brennan conceded that the Secretary had not actually used those words, but that the implication was the same (source: letter from Alf Jones, District Secretary, to Ben Gardner, General Secretary, 25 January 1951). Brennan did not call the meeting as the committee instructed, and indeed, the works committee, led by Brennan, urged the men in the West Works to return to work. His view was that attempting to make an issue of the dismissal could only jeopardise the relationships between the works committee and the Metropolitan-Vickers management. In addition, the local Stretford Branch of the ETU, containing 1,500 members (many at Metropolitan-Vickers) declared itself against the strike. Two important sources of legitimation for Bert Brennan's approach may be observed here. First, as was noted in Chapter 2, shop stewards may need to preserve the relationship with management if they are to retain the support of the instrumentally oriented members in the plant. Secondly, support came from the other main union on the works committee.

The District Secretary wrote to Brennan instructing that no sub-committee minutes of the works committee meetings were to be signed until the matter had been discussed with officials, so that their case should not be weakened at Central Conference (Works and Local Conferences having registered failure to agree), as Benny Rothman claimed that the minutes were inaccurate. The secretary of the works committee was also told this over the phone, but nevertheless Brennan and the works committee secretary allowed the minutes to be accepted.

In the West Works a strike committee was formed, backed by the district committee, and a number of pamphlets entitled 'Unity' were issued in support of the strike. On 26 November a special meeting of all AEU shop stewards at Metropolitan-Vickers was addressed by the Divisional Organiser and District Secretary. Estimates of the number on strike varied from 2,800 claimed by the strike committee to 654 claimed by the management. It is clear, however, that the attempt to spread the strike had failed. Indeed, the works committee now declared itself united in support of the dismissal of Rothman. By the end of November work had been resumed. The passive membership had exercised an arbitral role by refusing to go on strike and had registered their support for the Convener and the works committee.

On 17 January the no. 1 sub-committee held an inquiry into what had happened at Metropolitan-Vickers, particularly with reference to the failure of the strike. Summoned to attend were the AEU Convener (Bert Brennan) and the secretary of the works committee plus Benny Rothman and a witness in his favour. The meeting began by considering the letter from the District Secretary to the Convener, stating that no sub-committee minutes of works committee meetings held in the factory should be agreed with the employers until the matter had been discussed with the officials. Brennan replied that the minutes referred to had been accepted as a correct record by the negotiating sub-committee, by the workers' side of the works committee, and by the chief stewards of the five unions concerned. There is a clear implication that he considered this to be more than sufficient to accept the minutes without consulting the officers. It would appear that there was very little the no. 1 sub-committee could do about it. The meeting then moved on to consider why Brennan had refused the instruction to hold a mass meeting.

He said that Cliff Renshaw and John Crawford (both militant shop stewards at Metropolitan-Vickers and district committee members) had contacted him the morning after the district committee meeting and told him of the decision. He was under the impression that they had brought the message from the District Secretary but later found that this was not true. Cliff Renshaw said that he felt Brennan should be made aware of the committee's decision before he got a garbled report from workers in the shop who had attended the meeting (and John Crawford supported this). A member of the ETU was present in the stewards' room at the time and Cliff Renshaw had not been prepared to discuss the decision of the committee in his presence.

Bert Brennan agreed that the District Secretary did not use the words 'to gain support for our members in dispute' but claimed that the 'inference' of the resolution was to gain support, and it was for this reason that he felt unable to justify holding the meeting. In reply to questions he said that he felt he could have negotiated the reinstatement of Rothman if the men had returned to work, though he had to agree that others had taken part in the irregular action for which only Rothman was dismissed. The secretary of the works committee supported Brennan's argument, though the witness for Benny Rothman said he was fully satisfied that it was victimisation. When Rothman argued that Brennan had initially agreed that it was victimisation Brennan replied that this was because he had been misinformed by a number of members, including Rothman.

Brennan was asked if he would attend the district office when requested by the officials to discuss points made by the employers at the Local Conference, and he replied by saying that he was a member of the union and was always prepared to comply with the rules of the society.

The sub-committee then passed the following resolutions:

> That this committee reaffirms the decision already taken by the district committee that Rothman was victimised by his dismissal under the circumstances and the evidence considered tonight.

> That this committee, having heard the statements by Brother Brennan are fully satisfied that the District

Secretary at no stage instructed the Convener to call a meeting 'with a view to gaining support for our members in dispute'.

Failing to get a satisfactory decision at Central Conference on this case the district committee review the future supply of labour to Metropolitan-Vickers including dilution.

That at the appropriate time the District Secretary and Divisional Organiser attend a meeting of AEU shop stewards with a view to strengthening the organisation and explaining the position of the district committee and officials in this matter.

Legitimation from management, from other stewards on the works committee and contingent legitimation from the membership (except those in the West Works) supported the Convener in this dispute. It is clear that the competition was arbitrated in the Convener's favour by the other stewards and by the majority of the passive membership in the plant.

The Convener later received support from the Executive Council as well. Early in December the Executive Council were willing to pay the dispute benefit to the members who had stopped work, and a full wage benefit (equal to the 'district rate' and payable when a job had been lost as a consequence of union business) to Benny Rothman. But on 19 December they sent a letter refusing to pay the benefit, basing their decision on the report of the dispute sent to them by Brennan. In this letter they said that they felt the men were unwise not to follow the advice of their own elected representatives and to grant benefit would be tantamount to a repudiation of the advice which the works committee gave. The Executive Council did later relent, however, and paid dispute benefit, but the case itself was never resolved in Rothman's favour.

The Convener and managerial legitimation

At several points reference has been made to the way in which managements and conveners or stewards develop a working relationship, perhaps giving each an interest in protecting the power of the other. Another, though not in itself very important, incident may be useful to illustrate the strains created in the relationship between district committee and Convener by the Convener's perceived need to maintain the support of management for his role.

On 24 February 1952 a letter from the Salford 4th Branch was considered by the no. 2 sub-committee. A member of the branch, H. Wrigley, had been late returning to work at Metropolitan-Vickers after one hour's extension to the dinner break on 24 December, and the firm had refused to pay him for the two statutory holidays. The Convener's observations had been requested and these stated that the works committee had negotiated for the whole factory to have one hour's allowable lateness on Christmas Eve, and as all workers knew the penalty for lateness beforehand the works committee could not support the claim. The district committee resolved: 'That we instruct the Convener to register "failure to agree" in order that application for a Works Conference can be made.' However, Brennan did not register 'failure to agree'. When the case was reconsidered by the no. 3 sub-committee two months later he told them that he had been informed by Mr Main, the Assistant Works Manager, that if the case of Wrigley was pressed the concession would be withdrawn for the whole works in future. The reason for the delay, he said, was in using to their limits all the procedural agreements in the factory. The sub-committee considered the position and resolved: 'That this committee regret the delay of correspondence in answer to the letter of 25 February but in view of the statements made we await a full report of the position to date.' An amendment, 'That we accept Brother Brennan's explanation of this case' was defeated, and the resolution carried by five votes to two.

At the next meeting of the no. 3 sub-committee (on 1 May) the Convener's report was considered. This merely reiterated that management had stated that if the matter went into the procedure the concession would be withdrawn. The sub-committee resolved: 'That the district committee reaffirm its previous decision to instruct the Convener to register "failure to agree".' Voting on the resolution was two in favour and two against, and it was declared carried by the Chairman.

Three weeks later Brennan resigned from the district committee, giving as his reason pressure of work and responsibility to wife and family. In a letter to the district committee he said that he would always assist them to the best of his ability and perhaps at some later date he would rejoin. In the Divisional Organiser's report to the district committee of 10 July 1952 was the item: 'Metropolitan-

Vickers – Works Conference on claim for Christmas holiday pay to a member was not successful.'

The dispute – phase II

Though there were minor disputes in the intervening years the next important conflict between the district committee and some members of the now AEI works committee occurred in 1964.

A system of four twelve-hour shifts was introduced at the factory, and the district committee insisted that this system must stop. The Convener was summoned for a breach of the National Agreement but returned the summons. In view of this refusal to discuss the problem the shop stewards and members at the factory were instructed to cease the practice, shop stewards who failed to do so being threatened with the withdrawal of their credentials.

However, this dispute was not followed up, for in May 1964 it was followed by a more serious dispute which turned out to be an almost exact repeat of the Rothman case of 1951. This time the man dismissed was Cliff Renshaw, a member of both the district committee and the works committee, and considered to be one of the more militant of the AEI shop stewards. Frank Parker, another militant shop steward from AEI, on both of the committees, gave the district committee his version of what had happened.

Cliff Renshaw and three other members were having a chat on the shop floor when the Superintendant approached and asked what they were doing. Renshaw replied 'passing the time of day', but when the Superintendent asked another worker, a stone trimmer, he replied, 'trade union business'. According to Frank Parker all four workers were dismissed for this. The case was reported to the Convener and, again according to Frank Parker, it was at Bert Brennan's instigation that Cliff Renshaw was given a week's notice. A meeting of members in B Aisle (where the problem arose) decided to place the matter in the hands of the works committee. A sub-committee was set up of five representatives from each of the management and workers' sides but no progress was made. The firm claimed that if the men had been alert they would have seen the Superintendent approach, and in the interests of maintaining discipline the dismissals would have to stand. On 12 May a meeting of the members (about 500) in B Aisle was held and they decided to withdraw their labour, though Brennan urged them to remain at work.

A case study in arbitrated outcomes

The district committee meeting, held on the evening of the twelfth resolved:

> That this district committee considers the members concerned were wrongfully dismissed and in the case of Brother Renshaw his discharge constitutes victimisation. We therefore endorse the actions of our members at AEI in withdrawing their labour and instruct the District President and District Secretary to contact our shop stewards for full support of all AEU members in the factory.
>
> We request Executive Council to give official recognition to this dispute and to protest to the Engineering Employers' Federation against the actions of this firm.
>
> That we call upon Executive Council to give permission to operate Rule 13 Clause 15 for a local levy.
>
> That the District Secretary be empowered to call a special district committee meeting.

The following day (13 May) the management sent out telegrams to a number of strikers (estimates as to how many received these varied between 200 and 400). The telegram read:

> 4.5 pm
> Due to your unofficial action not supported by the Works Committee unless you present yourself for work at 7.45 am tomorrow it will be accepted that you have terminated your employment.
>
> Paterson, Works Manager

That evening the special meeting of the district committee was held, at which a deputation of shop stewards from AEI gave a report on the dispute. After considerable discussion the following resolutions were passed:

> We reiterate the district committee decision of 12 May 1964 that all our members be instructed to withdraw their labour.
>
> That the decisions of this district committee be conveyed to the Convener for the attention of all AEU shop stewards.

> We condemn the telegram sent to members by the
> company as denying a fundamental Trade Union right in
> the right to withdraw labour.

> An approach be made to the ETU for a joint factory
> meeting to be held on Friday 15 May at 12.15 pm.

> A letter be sent to the Confederation district committee
> explaining the decisions of the district committee.

By 14 May estimates of how many men were on strike varied from
4,000 (the union estimate) to 2,300 (the management estimate). On
the 15th a lunch-time meeting of all 12,000 manual workers was held
to vote on whether to stage a mass walkout. About 6,000 people
turned up to the meeting though management claimed that these
included 'many sightseers, staff employees, and people from neighbouring factories'. However, the meeting voted in favour of a full
stoppage and on the 16th a strike committee was set up.[2] On the
following Monday (18th) estimates of how many were on strike
varied between 10,000 (*Daily Worker*), 6,000 (unions) and 3,000
(management). The management continued to blame 'unusual
outside pressures' for the strike, saying 'management and work-
people alike remain mystified at these persistent outside attempts to
intervene in a purely domestic issue'.[3] By 'outside' the management
was referring particularly to the district committees of the AEU and
the ETU, although the strike was also backed by the district
committee of the Confederation of Shipbuilding and Engineering
Unions.

On 18 May the works committee made its opposition to the strike
clearly known. Nearly 500 copies of a statement issued by the works
committee were put up all over the factory. These read: 'The Works
Committee dissociates itself from the self-styled AEI strike committee and recommends all workers to return to work forthwith to enable
the dispute to be dealt with through the proper domestic and national
procedure.'

On 19 May another call was made to extend the strike from the
7,000 which the union estimated were on strike to all 12,000 workers
in the factory. At this meeting strikers called for the credentials of the
works committee stewards to be withdrawn, and Bob Wright,
secretary of the Confederation district committee, commented that as
seven members of the works committee had joined the strike the
works committee could not issue statements with full authority.

The works committee stewards had also refused to comply with a summons to meet the Confederation district committee 'to agree a common policy'.

It was on the 20th that the deadlock was broken when the management cancelled the dismissal telegrams to the strikers. Their withdrawal, said Bob Wright, meant that the main obstacle to a resumption of work had been removed. On Thursday 21 May the strikers accepted a recommendation from the strike committee and union officials to return to work, with the case of the four men dismissed to be dealt with through the procedural system. As far as the strike is concerned, like the one in 1951 it must be judged a failure. Although the union officials claimed that no 'climb-down' was involved in returning to work the situation was exactly as it would have been if no strike had taken place, the issue being dealt with through the procedure (a procedure which the events of 1951 and 1952 had shown was unlikely to give the union much satisfaction).

After the strike the district committee tried to get the Convener to attend a meeting to give an account of what had happened but each time he refused. For six months he refused to co-operate in any way with the district committee, sending in no shop stewards' quarterly reports and replying only by letter to the numerous demands that he attend the district committee or have his credentials withdrawn. On one occasion he wrote: 'I will not be in attendance to consider this matter as I consider this to be ultra vires as far as you are concerned.' And on another: 'I am in receipt of your summons to which I replied on 28 August 1964; as I am not aware of any other dismissals no further comment is necessary, as I have previously stated.'

As in 1951, the district committee got no support from the Executive Council, nor did the Confederation district committee. The Confederation committee had asked the National Executive of the Confederation to investigate the way that the union side of the works committee had behaved. The investigation was carried out by Bill Carron, the AEU President, and George Barnett, the General Secretary of the Confederation. However, they concluded that the Confederation district committee had exceeded their rights in backing the strike and organising meetings, and they had no criticisms of the works committee.

The Executive Council at first approved dispute benefit for the members who had gone on strike. At this Executive Council meeting were Bradley, Hanley, Berridge and Scanlon, giving the Council a 'left-wing' majority. They voted unanimously to approve benefit. The Council later reversed their decision at a second meeting when Scanlon was on annual leave and Carron, Boyd, Tallon and Lewis had returned from theirs, giving the Council a 'right-wing' majority. In response to the district committee's protest about this, the Executive Council replied that the matter was nothing to do with the district committee as the payment of benefits was a matter between branches and the Executive Council, district committees being informed for information purposes only.

The disputes procedure was then exhausted, 'failure to agree' having been recorded up to and including Central Conference level. When the district committee asked the Executive Council for permission to proceed into dispute with the firm this was refused on the grounds that the Executive Council wanted to be sure that a majority of members in the establishment would support the action.

Knowing that the district committee could not get the Convener to attend committee meetings (because the district committee had written to ask their advice), the Executive Council said they would only approve a ballot of the membership after the Convener had attended the district committee to be consulted. They then informed the committee that there was no provision, according to the rules, for summoning members before a sub-committee, though they could fine members for not complying with a summons to attend the full committee. (The district committee appealed against this ruling to the Final Appeal Court but lost.)

When the Convener again refused to attend a full committee meeting to consider further action at AEI the district committee again asked the Executive Council for advice and Hugh Scanlon (now Executive Council representative for Division 4) attended a sub-committee to discuss the whole question. At this meeting considerable discussion took place and it was resolved:

> Bearing in mind all the circumstances, and in the best interest of the membership we consider no useful purpose would be served in pursuing this matter. Shop stewards refusing to attend the district committee in future when summoned, this to be dealt with as provided for in Rule 13, Clause 4, lines 39–42.

This rule stated that members failing to attend, after being duly summoned, could be fined in such sum as the committee might determine, such fine not to exceed ten shillings.

Thus, even after the strike and the conflict between the district committee and the works committee the four sacked men did not get their jobs back, no sanctions were applied against Bert Brennan or the other shop stewards, and, if anything, the district committee was in a worse position since they had lost one of the rights they thought they had (to summon members compulsorily to sub-committee meetings).

The dispute – phase III

In 1967, AEI was taken over by the General Electric Company (GEC) and then merged with English Electric. The management began to pursue a programme of rationalisation in the factories of the new group. During the second half of the 1960s the number of manual workers at the Trafford Park works was reduced from 12,000 to 5,000 the bulk of the redundancies occurring as a result of the merger.

In response to expressions of concern from the branches the no. 1 sub-committee was delegated by the district committee in March 1968 to hold an enquiry into the possibility of redundancies. The Convener was summoned to attend but replied by letter, refusing to discuss the problem.

Branches were writing to the District Secretary detailing how the problem was affecting them; for example, two branches wrote to say that apprentices at AEI had been informed that they were liable to be made redundant on reaching 21. The district committee again summoned Brennan to attend but he replied that there was no problem to investigate and that he did not intend to be at the enquiry. The district committee resolved: 'That we are unable to accept that there are no problems relative to redundancy at AEI and Brother Brennan's refusal to attend the district committee and we impose a fine of ten shillings on Brother Brennan.'

Complaints about redundancy were still coming from the branches, so at the end of April the no. 1 sub-committee held another enquiry to which Bert Brennan was summoned, but again did not attend. At this enquiry it was reported that the Electronics Department at Trafford Park was undergoing a phased closure over a twelve-month period, involving about five hundred workers. The shop stewards had not taken steps to deal effectively with the position and overtime was being worked all over the factory, including that department. Another member stated that sixteen members had been made redundant in the Meter Department. Overtime was being worked and the Convener would not consider work-sharing. Yet another 'show cause' summons was sent to Brennan but he replied: 'Everything concerning redundancy is quite satisfactory inside the factory irrespective of what anyone may say outside the factory to the contrary . . . I therefore will not waste my time or yours by attending on the question.'

In May, Brennan was fined another ten shillings for failing to attend the district committee, and still the complaints from branches and members about redundancy at AEI kept reaching the district committee.

The AEU shop stewards at the Wythenshawe transformer factory decided, along with the stewards of the other unions, to form a separate Joint Shop Stewards Committee, unconnected with the works committee at Trafford Park. This was agreed by the district committee and by the Trafford Park works committee, and shortly after, the new Convener at Wythenshawe wrote to the district committee giving full details of the Company's policy relative to redundancy as it affected the Wythenshawe factory (about three hundred employees being involved).

In June, Brennan was fined another 10 shillings for failing to attend the district committee, and he also refused to attend a meeting of officials and shop stewards held to discuss a common policy at AEI. The district committee was forced to the conclusion that it had little option but to withdraw Brennan's credentials. On 18 June the no. 1 sub-committee resolved:

> Recognising the concern of a number of branches
> regarding redundancies at AEI/GEC Trafford Park and
> the inability of the district committee to take a decision
> because of the disregard of Brother Brennan for the
> district committee, we therefore charge that Brother
> Brennan has acted contrary to the interests of the
> membership and under Rule 13 be summoned down to
> show cause as to why he should not be disciplined.

The resolution was endorsed at the full district committee meeting the following week. When Brennan failed to attend the next full committee meeting (9 July) the district committee resolved unanimously: 'That the credentials of Brother Brennan as shop steward at AEI, Trafford Park be withdrawn.' And 'Subject to approval by the Executive Council of the above resolution a meeting be called of all AEU shop stewards at this works to elect a Convener.'

The meeting to elect a new Convener was held on 15 August. Forty-two shop stewards were present and a report was given of what had happened between the Convener and the district committee during the course of the year. Frank Parker (a member of the district committee) was elected as the new Convener, and three days later the district committee received a letter from the AEI management stating, 'we shall be pleased to grant Mr Parker the usual facilities for Convener in this factory'. It is difficult to assess precisely what this meant in terms of the relationship between the new Convener and the management. At face value it would seem to mean that Parker had received the legitimation of management.

However, other AEU shop stewards refused to co-operate with Parker, and less than two weeks after the election they were summoned to attend the no. 1 sub-committee to explain their refusal. Only one of the six AEU shop stewards on the works committee attended though Parker said he had issued summonses to them all. Two men had 'refused point-blank' to attend and the others had decided not to attend after some discussion. All five were issued with 'show cause' summonses but again refused to attend, and they were fined 10 shillings. A further resolution was passed to the effect that they be summoned to attend to 'show cause' why their shop stewards' credentials should not be withdrawn.

On 19 September the District Secretary received a letter from the Executive Council deploring the attitude of the shop stewards and suggesting that if they failed to carry out their undertaking in accordance with rule, they would consider action in accordance with Rule 13, Clause 10, lines 1–9 (that district committee resolutions be enforceable by a £5 fine, suspension from benefits, or expulsion from the union). This letter was read at the plant to the shop stewards concerned but they still refused to attend. Early in October 1967 the district committee resolved to withdraw their credentials and to hold a meeting of all AEU shop stewards at the works. At this meeting the five indicated their willingness to attend the district committee, so they were summoned once more. On the 29th they attended the no. 1 sub-committee to 'show cause' why their credentials should not be withdrawn. They explained that as works committee members they were in an awkward position. The Convener (Bert Brennan) had refused to attend the district committee as the works committee considered that the problem affected all unions in the factory and they felt they should support him in this issue. As they said they would support the district committee in future the sub-committee resolved: 'That we accept the assurance that shop stewards present will attend the district committee when summoned to do so. Under these circumstances we reverse the decision to withdraw their shop stewards' credentials.' The stewards' point illustrates the rival claims for the Convener's loyalty by the district committee and the works committee. The Convener chose to act as a representative of the multi-union workers' side of the works committee rather than as an AEU representative in the firm. According to the stewards he was thus entitled to receive, and got, their support in any dispute with the AEU hierarchy that this may have produced.

Even though the stewards agreed to support the district committee, Frank Parker continued to have 'difficulties' doing the job of Convener at Trafford Park. A further sub-committee enquiry was carried out at which Frank Parker, Bert Brennan and the other AEU members of works committee attended.

Brennan referred to the decision of the district committee in 1946 when the AEU and ETU had been in conflict. He quoted from the minutes: 'That the Works Committee shall be solely responsible for negotiations within the firm.' He had no intention of breaking rule, he said, the whole thing had been a misunderstanding and the organisation was bigger than himself. He stated that he would attend the district committee when summoned, and when asked by the Chairman if he was asking for the return of his credentials he said 'yes'. The sub-committee resolved:

> That we accept Brother Brennan's assurance that he would attend the district committee when summoned.

> That we accede to Brother Brennan's request to restore his credentials.

> That the district committee call a meeting of all

AEI/GEC shop stewards at an early date to report on district committee decisions.

This meeting was held at the end of November 1968 and Parker tendered his resignation as Convener. When the voting for the new Convener took place Bert Brennan was elected with 28 votes against Frank Parker's 10 votes. It is clear from these voting figures that Brennan continued to have support of the majority of AEU stewards in the plant. Though his statements at the meeting might appear to indicate a resolution of the competition in favour of the district committee it is clear that this meeting was only a face-saving exercise. The lack of support for the district committee's nominee as Convener was the crucial arbitral factor.

On 3 December a letter from the Executive Council was read to the full district committee meeting:

> The Executive council is gravely concerned at the reasoning of the members summoned from GEC/AEI Trafford Park. The plea that obligations to a body outwith the structure of this Union exempts such individuals from the authority of the district committee is completely unacceptable to the Executive Council.
>
> No member of our union can represent or act on behalf of our union, or its members, in any capacity, outwith the provisions of Rule 13 and the approval of Executive Council. Attention is drawn to Rule 13 Clause 10 which gives power to the district committee to pass resolutions on subject matters affecting the remainder of Rule 13 which, when approved by Executive Council, shall be binding upon all members working in the respective districts.
>
> Executive Council feel that there is no ambiguity about that phrase and attention should specifically be drawn to the fact that Rule 13, Clause 10 also provides for the enforcement of this clause by fine, suspension from benefits, or by expulsion.
>
> Referring to recent circumstances within GEC/AEI Trafford Park the Executive Council expects the district committee to act strictly in accordance with the provisions of Rule 13 Clause 10 should repetition of

these circumstances take place in future. The Executive
Council will not tolerate individuals or groups of
individuals seeking to undermine or set aside the authority
of the district committee. If such individuals have reason
to complain then there is adequate scope within Rule 20.
(*Rule 20 referred to the complaints and appeals procedure.*)

This letter from the Executive Council is of course in complete
contrast to the one they sent to the district committee on 19 December
1951, in which they refused to pay dispute benefit to the members who
had gone on strike, because they followed the instructions of the
district committee and not those of 'their elected representatives', the
works committee. However, this seems to be more a reflection of the
changing composition of the Executive Council than a conversion to
the notion of district committee authority on the part of the Council
members of 1951.

In January 1970 the Convener was criticised by the district
committee for the Christmas holiday arrangements and for a
piecework agreement negotiated by the works committee. In January
1971 the Convener was fined £5 for allowing the same Christmas
holiday arrangements to be implemented.

Though there were no dramatic confrontations in the intervening
years the Convener and works committee continued to go their own
way until Bert Brennan retired in 1977 at the age of 72. The vacuum
that his departure created was never properly filled, though the
position changed again in 1979 when the company reorganised the
site into five separate units, with five conveners.

Concluding comments

One of the first conclusions that emerges from the case study is that
the activities of the Convener and the AEU members of the works
committee were much more strongly directed towards the plant
organisation as a collectivity than towards the district committee,
although this generalisation should be modified in at least two ways.
First, it is notable that in the first few years of the study the Convener
(Bert Brennan) was a member of the district committee, both while
Hugh Scanlon was Convener (up to 1947) and then for a few years
after (up to 1952). As one of the shop stewards later expressed the
problem, a conflict between the district committee and the works

committee placed works committee members 'in an awkward position'. It would seem that by his membership Brennan must initially have been drawn towards both committees. It was after he became Convener and a conflict arose that the ties to the district committee became weak (so that he left) and he later appeared to become antagonistic as the conflict strengthened. The evidence is that Bert Brennan was strongly oriented towards the principle of collective organisation but that he saw this principle as best served by the plant organisation.

The second modification of the generalisation is that the AEU members of the works committee did not always represent a unified group. Usually there were some members from this committee sitting on the district committee and these too might be expected to face a problem of conflicting loyalties (for example, Cliff Renshaw, John Crawford and Frank Parker). From the evidence it would appear that these members were more strongly oriented to the district committee.

However, as the incidents progressed the antagonism between the two groups became greater and it would seem reasonable to say that the congruence between the decisions which the district committee tried to impose and the expectations of the works committee was extremely low. In the two dismissal cases the district committee's decision was to call a strike and this was opposed by the works committee, who preferred to negotiate.

The problem of legitimation of district committee decisions occurs at several points in the case study. The resolution passed in 1946 giving the works committee sole negotiating rights in the factory appears to have provided the Convener with at least a bureaucratic rationalisation for his actions. He could claim, as he did in 1968, that his actions were legitimated by this resolution and that the district committee and district officials had no right to intervene in negotiations within the factory.

As far as the application of sanctions is concerned it would appear to have been necessary to apply sanctions against the works committee members, and the Convener in particular, in each of the three main cases. However, they were not applied until the last case. This seems to be a reflection of the degree of independence which the plant organisation had developed. The problem of 'information flow' was not that the district committee received no accounts of events. These were related (though perhaps with some bias) almost as soon as they took place, and in the redundancy case a lot of information came from the branches. The problem was the lack of formal means of conveying district committee decisions to the Convener and works committee and, perhaps more importantly, to the membership in the plant. The Convener was in a much better position to receive the support of the membership because of his superior 'linkages' with them. The problems of multi-unionism and work-group support appear to have been much more important constraints on committee application of sanctions. The likelihood is that sanctions would have been ineffective. This proposition can be tested against the evidence of the last case (redundancies) where it can be seen that in the long run the sanctions *were* ineffective. The source of Bert Brennan's 'power' *vis-à-vis* the district committee appears to lie in the support which he received from other members of the works committee, from the majority of other AEU shop stewards in the plant, from the management, from the Executive Council and from the plant membership. Though it has not been revealed by the incidents in this case, it was suggested, in an interview, that when the plant dominated the district membership statistics, the district and even national full-time officers tended to seek Bert Brennan's favour for electoral support.

Until the district committee had applied sanctions against the other AEU members of the works committee it was not possible even to attempt to control the AEU section of the plant organisation. Although the immediate response was favourable in that Brennan and the other stewards asked for their credentials to be returned and agreed to abide by district committee decisions, the longer-term effect was less favourable.

The refusal to recognise the decisions of the district committee as legitimate stems from two sources: first from the belief that the district committee had no right to intervene in plant affairs – 'I consider this to be *ultra vires* as far as you are concerned' (Brennan, 1964), and secondly, that being elected directly by the work-force at the plant they had more right to control plant affairs; a view supported at the time by the Executive Council – 'the men were unwise not to follow the advice of their own elected representatives' (Executive Council, 1951).

In each of the three phases of the dispute the Convener received sufficient legitimation for his activities to achieve a favourable outcome. In the first strike incident he received the support of all the identifiable sources of legitimacy, and the passive membership arbitrated the dispute in his favour. In the second strike incident the district committee attempted to regain some legitimacy by obtaining the support of the multi-union district committee of the Confederation of Shipbuilding and Engineering Unions (CSEU) but legitimation was denied to this collectivity as well (for example, the report of enquiry into the dispute by the union leadership criticised the CSEU district committee for acting beyond its role). Although more of the membership followed the district committee's call, the management, some stewards, some of the membership, and the union leaderships were collectively too 'powerful' for the district committee. The case was again resolved in the Convener's favour.

The experience of these incidents contributed to the decision to withdraw credentials in the third incident. Not only had legitimacy broken down between the Convener and the district committee (as in all previous cases) but it had been shown that arbitrated outcomes had favoured the Convener. The application of sanctions thus represented an attempt to 'internalise' the outcome, by the production of a 'negotiated outcome'. Despite this intention the outcome was arbitrated by the other stewards on the works committee, who refused to co-operate with the district committee's nominated Convener. The sanctions were thus rendered ineffective. Similar findings were reported by Batstone *et al.* (1977). Looking at policy differences between full-time officers and the Joint Shop Stewards Committee they found that where a conveners' coalition disagreed with a full-time officers' coalition the conveners' coalition more frequently won the day.

7
Conclusions

Introduction

In the opening chapter of this book I suggested that the theorising on trade union government has not fully captured the essence of the political process, and that this failure can be attributed in part to the use of models which emphasise a dichotomy between a leadership and a membership, restricting debate to the relative incidence of oligarchy or democracy. The analysis and case studies of this book have sought to show that in one union at least this simple model is inappropriate, since union policies are both formed and played out in arenas at different levels of the organisation. Conflicts within a trade union can arise because the areas of jurisdiction are ill-defined, particularly where traditions of local autonomy run counter to the requirements of centralised administration. By looking from the perspective of a single level, that of the district committee, the case studies have been able to highlight the fragile balance of control between leadership, lower-level collectivities, and the rank and file.

Though the lack of detailed knowledge of how local union organisations actually operate is a regrettable hiatus for our understanding of trade unionism, the purpose of the case studies was not solely, or even primarily, an attempt to remedy this deficiency. Rather, the case studies have been used as settings in which to examine the ideas about the decision-making process. Any case study is bound to be idiosyncratic to some extent and the two contained in this study are obviously no exception. Nevertheless, they provide a useful basis from which to draw some tentative conclusions, first about the position of district committees and branches in the government of the AUEW(E), but more importantly about the nature of participation in trade unions and about trade union government in general.

Conclusions

The district in the AUEW(E)

Though the case of the Manchester district committee has been used in this book as an example of a particular phenomenon, rather than the object of study in its own right, there are a number of points about these committees which are worth re-emphasising. If the evidence of the case studies accurately depicts the relationship between the district committees and other collectivities in the AUEW(E) there are considerable grounds for questioning the widely held view that these committees possess 'too much power'. In Chapter 3 it was noted that criticisms by the Donovan Commission (1968) and the National Board for Prices and Incomes (1967) refer to the powers of the district committees as deriving from the traditions of the nineteenth century. It is clear from this study that though tradition may imbue the district committees with certain advantages for the exercise of power (for example, derived from rule), these advantages are severely limited by the weak structural linkages with those whom they would need to control (the membership) and by the existence of rival claimants to the legitimacy which the membership can grant. Although tradition may be one element in an authority relationship it is not sufficient on its own to explain why groups comply with decisions which they feel are against their interests. It would be closer to a correct appreciation of the role of tradition to suggest that district autonomy led to the creation and maintenance of an organisation structure in which few restraints are placed on the activities of district committees and, further, led to the provision of some sanctions for the enforcement of district policy. Even so, such an interpretation would tend to overestimate the committees' overall power.

It is equally misleading to suggest that district committees derive power from a bargaining role with employers. As has been noted, the committee members do not themselves negotiate but instruct and ratify the work of the local officials.

Warner (1972) suggested that attention should be directed at the 'new district centres of power which are developing' from a coalition between district committees and workshop organisations. While correctly seeing the district committee as 'a rival source of authority and influence to the headquarters of the national union', he tends to overstate the unity of interest between the committees and workshop organisations. As this study has shown, there is no more reason to suggest a unity of interest between the district committees and the shop stewards as opposed to the head office, than between any other of the hierarchical collectivities in the trade union. Indeed, a workshop organisation may find more common ground with the head office (to use Warner's expression) in competition with a district committee. The study does not suggest the district committees are powerless. Indeed, there are several means whereby they can gain control over the activities of workshop organisations. They can derive legitimate authority from the provisions of the rule book, and from the electoral and solidarity principles. The district committee can also offer the workshops some expertise, information, strike approval and perhaps also external legitimation in their dealings with management. Part of this 'service' is a fund of information about agreements, both local and national, which may be used for comparisons, and as a source of expertise for assessing agreements. Under rule, all agreements should be sent to the district committe for ratification, and it was suggested in an interview that only workshop organisations confident of not 'getting into a mess' with their agreements would risk ignoring this rule. The approval of strikes (if in turn ratified by the Executive Council) opens the way to the payment of dispute benefit to the strikers and to the levying of a district strike fund. This is a 'service' and should not be taken to mean that the district committee can control strikes. Boraston *et al.* found that only a fraction of the Leachester district's strikes came before the committee and hence the committee had little power to control strikes. In the event of legitimation and exchange power breaking down, negative sanctions may be wielded against workshop organisations, but this strategy is rare.

A further important source of control over the workshops derives from the relationship between the committee and district officers. The committee can 'instruct' the district officers in their negotiations, and the officers' work must be ratified by the committee before it can be finalised. Although the limited nature of this power has been pointed out, it nevertheless represents an important addition to the committee's means of control over the workshops. On balance, therefore, it can be argued that the district committees play an important role in the political process but this role is limited by a number of constraints.

How generalisable are such conclusions? Is the Manchester district typical of districts in the AUEW(E)? Certainly the evidence is broadly in line with the conclusions of Boraston *et al.*, who have conducted the only other study that examines local organisation in the AUEW(E) in any detail. They too found that there were plant organisations which the district committee found impossible to control. In one plant the Convener 'was openly at odds with many of the current members (of the district committee) . . ., handled all issues personally, and referred nothing to the district'. The Leachester district committee had policies on overtime, piece-work, productivity, redundancy and measured day work but: 'the committee and the shop stewards sub-committee could not impose these principles throughout the district. They could act only where their attention was drawn to a draft agreement or to excessive overtime working, and they had no effective means of ensuring that their decisions were carried out' (1975: 35). However, it can also be argued that the present study provides a warning that generalisations may be misleading. In the 'Leachester' district Boraston *et al.* found, as Derber (1955) had before them, that the district committee dominated the full-time officers. But whereas Derber tried to generalise this finding to the AEU as a whole, Boraston found that in the 'South Marlshire' district the full-time officers were dominant. There is little in the structure or the constitution of the union which can predict the relationship between districts and the other collectivities with which they deal. It is the process of bargaining, latent and manifest conflict, and the negotiation of order which determines those relationships, and this can only be discovered at first hand by a detailed analysis of issues and processes, conflict and conflict resolution.

The role of the branch

Current orthodoxy has it that the branch plays a negligible role in the activities of the AUEW. In terms of branch attendances and the extent of branch control over decision-making this proposition would seem to be valid. Hyman and Fryer state that 'few union branches genuinely function as instruments of intra-union democracy' (1975: 155).

Nevertheless, this study has identified a branch role which is worth re-emphasising. After workshop organisations as a source of information, district committees receive most information on plant activities from the branches. This information is often, though not always, concerned with members' complaints about the way in which shop stewards are handling either members' grievances or general policy issues. In the case study on the control of workshops it was seen that the main source of complaints against the Convener's handling of the redundancy issue was the branches. In this way the branches provide an important communication channel between the members and the district committee which serves to limit the autonomy of the workshop organisation. This role is made possible by the separate bases of branch (geographic) and workshop organisation. Those who argue that the branch should be based on the workplace should at least be aware that any gain in administrative or representative effectiveness may be at the expense of a further increase in the autonomy of shop stewards. Since it has been argued that the immediacy of the shop steward's relation with those he represents yields an approximation to primitive democracy such a move may be welcomed. However, to the extent that shop stewards may themselves be formed into bureaucracies which 'possess their own institutional interests, to be defended against membership as against management and unions' (Goodman and Whittingham, 1973: 127) there are grounds for arguing that some alternative channel of membership complaint is desirable.

McCarthy (1966) suggested that compared with the south of England, AEU branch life was more vigorous in the northern industrial areas where shop stewards were initially only a supplement to strongly organised branches. To the extent that this was true it may be argued that the observed use of the branches as a channel of complaint may reflect more active branch life in general, and that the observation, while not atypical, may be characteristic only of northern areas. However, Boraston *et al.* found that in the Midlands (an 'intermediate' area on McCarthy's branch activity scale) the branch is widely used by the dissatisfied member to draw attention to the handling of an issue within a plant. The particular conclusion is that the branch, far from being completely redundant as an element in the polyarchy, plays an important mediating role in relationships between district committees, shop stewards' organisations, and the membership.

If it is true that the branch is becoming increasingly moribund, and the evidence of branches in the Manchester district in the 1970s suggests that it is, then substantial problems are raised for the union. The myth is still perpetuated that the branch is the basis of the organisation, the member's chief link with the union. The branches are still responsible for the collection of contributions and for the claiming and payment of sickness and strike benefits, legal aid and other services. Branches which become inefficient through low attendance and inability to attract branch officers cease to provide members with the services that they require and this can only do damage to the long-term viability of the union. Both for reasons of government and of viability it is important to the union that branch life is in some way revitalised.

Participation and government

The opening chapter raised a number of questions about how trade unions reconcile conflicting interests amongst members, manage dissent, and indeed asked what is actually meant by popular control over decision-making. The present study, while not providing complete answers to such broad questions, allows a number of insights into these internal processes of government. One of the main themes in the literature on union government is the apparent conflict between efficient organisation and rank-and-file control over decision-making. As has been suggested, the Webbs and Michels took a relatively pessimistic view of this problem, and this tendency has pervaded the literature to this day, supported even from within the trade unions themselves. Seidman *et al.* (1958: 211) quoted John L. Lewis, the American United Mine Workers leader, at the union's convention in 1936: 'It is a question of whether you desire your organisation to be the most effective instrumentality within the realm of possibility for a labour organisation or whether you prefer to sacrifice the efficiency of your organisation in some respects for a little more academic freedom in the selection of some local representatives in a number of districts.'

However, there are a number of reasons why 'representation' and 'administration' need not be conflicting objectives. For administration to be effective a high level of participation is required since unions rely heavily on the contributions of unpaid helpers. These activists, who become shop stewards and sit on the district committees, the divisional committees and the National Committee, expect that their participation will be rewarded by a share in the decision-making process of the union. It is not surprising, therefore, that activists at all levels will seek to maximise their share in this decision-making, and that this leads to the conflicts which have been described as characteristic of trade union governments. It can also be seen that these conflicts are as likely to be between groups of activists as between the rank and file and the leadership. It is through this process of negotiating over decisions that some of the conflicting interests can be reconciled and dissenting opinions voiced.

There is, though, another important aspect to participation. The rank and file, while not occupying active roles in the union, nevertheless participate in the process whereby opinions are formed and activists influenced in the positions they adopt. Most importantly, as has been shown, the rank and file register their support for those activists that they perceive to be best representing their interests. Administrative control is enhanced by the extent to which the rank and file identify with the policies pursued, and this is most likely where there exists a form of government in which activists are made responsive to the interests of the rank and file. Problems of dissent arise either when the rank and file are denied the opportunity to influence activists and to arbitrate conflicts, or when the interests of different groups of the rank and file are so heterogeneous that no compromise is possible. It is this latter situation that provokes the breakaway trade union, even when its chances of success are not high.

In the AUEW(E) there are a number of ways in which dissent may be expressed.[1] The electoral process is sufficiently robust for Edelstein and Warner to suggest that the union is democratic. The constitution provides for checks and balances on the authority of the national leadership, giving scope to lower-level collectivities to exercise a degree of independence, as seen in the internal struggles between the national leadership and the districts and between the national leadership and the shop stewards. This study has shown that this process goes further than the periodic disputes between the national leadership and other collectivities or the rank and file. The lower-level collectivities themselves can come into conflict and as the second case study suggests, they seek the support of the rank and file for their policies. Compliance with the appeals of one group rather than another is thus a significant additional mechanism whereby 'popular control' can be achieved. Rank-and-file involvement is likely to be greatest in those areas which are seen to be the most relevant for the satisfaction of their immediate interests. Where decision-making is diffused among a number of different levels in the union hierarchy then so too must be an effective representative system. Decisions made at the plant level by shop stewards' committees (or by full-time officers) would suggest a different system of representation from that required by centralised decision-making and hence members will attach different meanings to the formal representative structure (for example, the delegate conference). Evidence from the United States suggests greater rank-and-file involvement in those local unions with important decision-making powers, and, in, the UK, Goldthorpe *et al.* provide evidence of active membership participation in decision-making at shop-floor level.

As was seen in the second case study, the rank and file may thus have different orientations to different collectivities (for example, the work group, the plant or local organisation) and it is these orientations which will influence, and be influenced by, the degree of participation.

Trade union government

This study reinforces the view that conflict in trade unions is the rule rather than the exception. What it attempts to show is that conflict arises in a number of arenas within a union, not merely at the level of the leadership. It may be that the notion of interdependent collectivities pursuing their own interests, sometimes convergent, sometimes divergent, within an overall framework of rules is particularly appropriate to the AUEW(E) where in one form or another, such questions have dominated internal political life. Similarly detailed studies in other unions are necessary to see how general are the findings of this study, particularly studies of those general unions descended from the 'New Unionism' phase of union growth in the late nineteenth century. It may be that the greater degree of centralisation in these general unions does indeed tend to focus dissent into a conflict between the union's leaders and the whole or part of its rank and file. Nevertheless, the last ten to fifteen years have seen even these unions moving away from centralised forms of government towards limited forms of local autonomy as a response to shifts in the pattern of bargaining. The TGWU has always tried to absorb the diversity of interests through its trade group structure, though not always successfully, as the dispute between lorry drivers and docker members of the union over containerisation indicated. Under Jack Jones the union made a strenuous effort at devolution, setting up advisory district committees cutting across the trade group boundaries, and giving encouragement to the union's shop stewards. Similarly the GMWU's constitutional changes in 1975 set up a new tier of district full-time officers reflecting the growing pressures towards devolution following the trauma of events like the unofficial strike of glass workers at Pilkington's in St Helens in 1970.

Hawkins (1981) refers to the changes in both these unions as 'pragmatic devolution', and though the moves to devolution are led from the top (and can hardly be described as conferring local autonomy) the trend is clearly away from the rigidly centralised forms of government of the past. In terms of the dichotomy traditionally employed this would certainly make these unions less oligarchic, but will it make them more democratic? The evidence from unions like the AUEW suggests not. It may be that some additional way of looking at union government in general is required which concentrates on how union members collectively formulate a view of their interests and seek to reconcile their differences through bargaining. The argument of this book is not that the concept of polyarchy alone can satisfy this requirement but that when it is placed alongside the concepts of democracy and oligarchy the theorising on trade union government is no longer unnecessarily limited. Hyman (1975) has asked whether a polyarchic trade union can also be democratic. The probability is that it cannot; it may even be difficult to distinguish from Michels' competing oligarchies. Nevertheless, concern for what is felt ought to be the situation should not be allowed to limit the range of concepts and techniques which are appropriate to describing and analysing the situation as it actually exists.

Notes

Chapter 3 Polyarchy in the engineering section of the AUEW

1 At the delegate meeting of 1912 it was decided to reduce the size of the Executive Council to seven members. The Executive Council opposed this move but after a short struggle (during which the Council locked themselves in the union's offices) a new Executive Council was elected.
2 Though the conference generally meets once a year the National Committee can 'call itself into being', in the form of additional or recall conferences.
3 *National Committee Report* (1961).
4 *National Committee Report* (1953).
5 *Guardian*, 20 September 1961.
6 *AEU Monthly Journal*, June 1966.

Chapter 4 The Manchester district committee

1 For example, Lipset *et al.* (1956) Tannenbaum and Kahn (1958) Sayles and Strauss (1967).
2 A remark in an interview, ascribed to a convener who was having difficulties with the committee.
3 District committee standing orders, p. 5.
4 The issues of wages, overtime, demarcation, dilution, redundancy and shop steward organisation appear to be the main preoccupations of the sub-committees throughout the study period.
5 Though, strictly speaking, the rules only legitimate the summoning of members to full committee meetings.
6 Usually a short, miscellaneous, category of committee business, only rarely containing items of importance.
7 In practice, to the administrative assistant to the Executive Council member of the electoral division. They are only referred to the member himself if a query arises, and only to the full Council if very important issues of policy or principle are raised.

8 Which limits committee activity to specific trade questions, and shop stewards' organisation. This has been changed to Rule 12 in the latest revisions to the union Rule Book.
9 Though the actual administration of the benefit is through the branches.
10 For example, in 1950 the Executive Council got the TGWU to agree that they had wrongly recruited AEU members at the Manchester Corporation Transport Department.
11 For example, the minutes of 22 June 1965 contain a letter from the Executive Council referring to negotiations at Manchester Airport (affecting more than one district), and those of 20 January 1970 a letter referring to negotiations for decentralised bargaining at Massey Ferguson (conducted nationally).
12 In the smaller districts the District Secretary is part-time.
13 Boraston *et al.* (1975: 16) estimate that in the smaller of the two districts they studied, administration took up about 20 per cent of the secretary's time.
14 'District Committees may enter into negotiations with employers in their respective districts with a view to having shops worked exclusively by the members of the Union' (Rule 12 Clause 12).
15 Sub-committee minutes, 18 June 1968.

Chapter 5 The district committee and the Executive Council: a case study in negotiated outcomes

1 District committee minutes (1953). Unless otherwise attributed all quotations in this and the succeeding chapter are from committee minutes.
2 Openshaw was the Executive Councilman with responsibility for the Manchester district.

Chapter 6 The district committee and a workshop organisation: a case study in arbitrated outcomes

1 For the managerial and financial background to these mergers see Jones and Marriott (1972).
2 An account of the strike and details of the composition of the Committee was published as *AEI Voice* No. 1, May–June 1964 and *AEI Voice* No. 2, June-July 1964.
3 *Guardian*, 19 May 1964.

Chapter 7 Conclusions

1 Though it is worth noting that several breakaways from the AEU were attempted in the 1940s and 1950s.

Select bibliography

Abell, P. (ed.) (1975) *Organizations as Bargaining and Influence Systems*, London: Heinemann
(1977) 'The Many Faces of Power and Liberty: Revealed Preference, Autonomy and Teleological Explanation', *Sociology* 11, pp. 3–24
Allen, V. (1954) *Power in Trade Unions*, London: Longman
(1971) *The Sociology of Industrial Relations*, London: Longman
Amalgamated Engineering Union (AEU) (1968) *The Evidence of the AEU to the Royal Commission on Trade Unions and Employers Associations*, London: HMSO
Amalgamated Union of Engineering Workers (AUEW) (1980) *Rule Book*, London: AUEW
Arnison, J. (1970) *The Million Pound Strike*, London: Lawrence and Wishart
Bachrach, P. and Baratz, M. (1962) 'The Two Faces of Power', *American Political Science Review* 56, pp. 947–52
(1963) 'Decisions and Non-decisions', *American Political Science Review* 57, pp. 641–51
(1970) *Power and Poverty: Theory and Practice*, Oxford: Oxford University Press
Bain, G. (1972) 'The Employers' Role in the Growth of White-Collar Unionism', in McCarthy, W. (ed.) *Trade Unions*, Harmondsworth: Penguin, pp. 255–73
Banks, J. (1974) *Trade Unionism*, London: Collier–Macmillan
Barkin, S. (1954) 'Labour Unions and Workers' Rights in Jobs', in Kornhouser, A., Dubin, R. and Ross, A. (eds.) *Industrial Conflict*, London: McGraw Hill, pp. 121–31
Batstone, E., Boraston, I. and Frenkel, S. (1977) *Shop Stewards in Action*, Oxford: Blackwell
Bealey, F. (1977) 'The Political System of the Post Office Engineering Union', *British Journal of Industrial Relations* 15, pp. 374–95
Beynon, H. (1973) *Working for Ford*, London: Allen Lane
Boraston, I., Clegg, H. and Rimmer, M. (1975) *Workplace and Union*, London: Heinemann

119

Bibliography

Brooks, D. (1975) *Race and Labour in London Transport*, Oxford: Oxford University Press

Brown, W. (ed.) (1981) *The Changing Contours of British Industrial Relations*, Oxford: Blackwell

Burgess, K. (1975) *The Origins of British Industrial Relations*, London: Croom Helm

Carew, A. (1976) *Democracy and Government in European Trade Unions*, London: George Allen and Unwin

Chamberlain, N. W. (1951) *Collective Bargaining*, New York: McGraw Hill

Child, J., Loveridge, R. and Warner, M. (1973) 'Towards an Organizational Study of Trade Unions', *Sociology* 7, pp. 71–91

Clegg, H. (1954) *General Union*, Oxford: Blackwell

(1970) *The System of Industrial Relations in Great Britain*, Oxford: Blackwell

(1976) *Trade Unionism under Collective Bargaining*, Oxford: Blackwell

Clegg, H. and Adams, R. (1957) *The Employers' Challenge*, Oxford: Blackwell

Clegg, H., Killick, A. and Adams, R. (1961) *Trade Union Officers*, Oxford: Blackwell

Clegg, S. (1975) *Power, Rule and Domination*, London: George Allen and Unwin

(1977) 'Power, Organization Theory, Marx and Critique', in Clegg, S. and Dunkerley, D. (eds.) *Critical Issues in Organizations*, London: Routledge and Kegan Paul, pp. 21–40

Coates, K. and Topham, A. (1970) *Workers' Control*, London: Panther

Cole, G. D. H. (1973) *Workshop Organization*, London: Hutchinson

Coleman, J. R. (1960) 'The Compulsive Pressures of Democracy in Unionism' in Galenson, W. and Lipset, S. M. (eds.) *Labour and Trade Unionism*, London: Wiley, pp. 207–15

Cook, A. H. (1963) *Union Democracy – Practice and Ideal*, Ithaca, New York: Cornell University Press

Crozier, M. (1964) *The Bureaucratic Phenomenon*, Chicago: University of Chicago Press

Cyriax, G. and Oakeshott, R. (1960) *The Bargainers*, London: Faber

Dahl, R. (1957) 'The Concept of Power', *Behavioural Science* 2 pp. 201–15

(1961) *Who Rules? Democracy as Power in an American City*, New Haven: Yale University Press

(1971) *Polyarchy, Participation and Opposition*, New Haven: Yale University Press

Dahrendorf, R. (1959) *Class and Class Conflict in Industrial Society*, Stanford: Stanford University Press

Dash, J. (1970) *Good Morning Brothers*, London: Mayflower

Bibliography

Dean, L. (1958) 'Interaction, Reported and Observed: The Case of One Local Union', *Human Organization* 17, pp. 36–44

Derber, M. (1955) *Labour–Management Relations at the Plant Level under Industry-Wide Bargaining*, Preoria: University of Illinois Press

Donaldson, L. and Warner, M. (1974) 'Bureaucratic and Electoral Control in Occupational Interest Associations', *Sociology* 8, pp. 47–57

Donovan, Lord (1968) Chairman, Royal Commission on Trade Unions and Employers' Associations, *Report*, London: HMSO

Edelstein, J. D. (1967) 'An Organizational Theory of Union Democracy', *American Sociological Review* 32, pp. 19–39

Edelstein, J. D., Warner, M. and Cooke, W. (1970) 'The Pattern of Opposition in British and American Unions', *Sociology* 4, pp. 145–63

Edelstein, J. D. and Warner, M. (1971) 'On Measuring and Explaining Union Democracy', *Sociology* 5, pp. 398–400

(1975) *Comparative Union Democracy*, London: George Allen and Unwin

Edwards, C. (1978) 'Measuring Union Power: A Comparison of Two Methods Applied to the Study of Local Union Power in the Coal Industry', *British Journal of Industrial Relations* 16, pp. 1–15

Eldridge, J. E. T. (1968) *Industrial Disputes*, London: Routledge and Kegan Paul

(1971) *Sociology and Industrial Life*, London: Michael Joseph

Fay, S. (1970) *Measure for Measure*, London: Chatto and Windus

Flanders, A. (1968) *Trade Unions*, London: Hutchinson

(1970) *Management and Unions*, London: Faber

Fletcher, R. (undated) *Problems of Union Democracy*, Institute of Workers' Control Pamphlet Series, 21, Nottingham: Institute of Workers' Control

(1970) 'Trade Union Democracy – Structural Factors', in Coates, K., Topham, A. and Brown, M. B. (eds.) *Trade Union Register*, London: Merlin, pp. 73–85

(1973) 'One Union for the Engineering Industry, Trade Union Ideology and the Rule Book', in Brown, M. B. and Coates, K. (eds.) *Trade Union Register No. 3*, Nottingham: Spokesman Books

Fox, A. (1971) *A Sociology of Work in Industry*, London: Collier–Macmillan

Fox, A. and Flanders, A. (1969) 'The Reform of Collective Bargaining: From Donovan to Durkheim', *British Journal of Industrial Relations* 7, pp. 151–80

French, J. and Raven, B. (1959) 'The Bases of Social Power', in Cartwright, D. (ed.) *Studies in Social Power*, Ann Arbor: University of Michigan Press, pp. 150–67

Goldstein, J. (1952) *The Government of British Trade Unions*, London: George Allen and Unwin

Bibliography

Goldthorpe, J., Lockwood, D., Bechhofer, F. and Platt, J. (1968) *The Affluent Worker: Industrial Attitudes and Behaviour*, Cambridge: Cambridge University Press

Goodman, J. and Whittingham, T. (1973) *Shop Stewards* London: Pan

Gouldner, A. (1954) *Patterns of Industrial Bureaucracy*, Glencoe, Illinois: Free Press

Government Social Survey (1968) *Workplace Industrial Relations*, London: HMSO

Gramsci, A. (1968) 'Soviets in Italy', *New Left Review* 51, pp. 28–58

Gretton, J. (1971) 'How are Trade Unions Reshaping Themselves?', *New Society* 17, pp. 348–51

Hall, K. and Miller, I. (1971) 'Industrial Attitudes to Skill Dilution' *British Journal of Industrial Relations* 9, pp. 1–20

Hawkins, K. (1981) *Trade Unions*, London: Hutchinson

Hemingway, J. (1978) *Conflict and Democracy: Studies in Trade Union Government*, Oxford: Oxford University Press

Hinton, J. (1973) *The First Shop Stewards' Movement*, London: George Allen and Unwin

Hobbes, T. (1946) *Leviathan*, Oxford: Blackwell

Hoxie, R. F. (1923) *Trade Unionism in the United States*, New York: Appleton

Hughes, J. (1967) *Trade Union Structure and Government*, Royal Commission Research Paper 5, London: HMSO

Hyman, R. (1971a) *The Workers' Union*, Oxford: University Press

(1971b) *Marxism and the Sociology of Trade Unionism*, London: Pluto Press

(1972) *Strikes*, London: Fontana

(1975) *Industrial Relations: A Marxist Introduction*, London: Macmillan

(1978) 'Pluralism, Procedural Consensus and Collective Bargaining', *British Journal of Industrial Relations* 16 pp. 16–40

Hyman, R. and Brough, I. (1975) *Social Values and Industrial Relations* Oxford: Blackwell

Hyman, R. and Fryer, B. (1975) 'Trade Unions', in McKinlay, J. (ed.) *Processing People*, London: Holt, Rhinehart and Winston, pp. 150–213

Jefferys, J. B. (1946) *The Story of the Engineers*, London: Lawrence and Wishart

Jones, R. and Marriott, O. (1972) *Anatomy of a Merger*, London: Pan

Lane, T. and Roberts, K. (1971) *Strike at Pilkingtons*, London: Fontana

Lerner, S. (1961) *Breakaway Unions and the Small Trade Union*, London: George Allen and Unwin

Lester, R. A. (1966) *As Unions Mature*, Oxford: Oxford University Press

Lipset, S. M. (1960) 'The Political Process in Trade Unions', in Galenson, W. and Lipset, S. M. (eds.) *Labour and Trade Unionism*, London: Wiley, pp. 216–42

Bibliography

Lipset, S. M., Trow, M. and Coleman, J. (1956) *Union Democracy*, Glencoe, Illinois: Free Press

Lukes, S. (1974) *Power: A Radical View*, London: Macmillan

McCarthy, W. E. J. (1966) *The Role of Shop Stewards in British Industrial Relations*, Royal Commission Research Paper 1, London: HMSO

McCarthy, W. E. J. and Parker, S. R. (1968) *Shop Stewards and Workshop Relations*, Royal Commission Research Paper 10, London: HMSO

Marcus, P. M. (1964) 'Organizational Change: The Case of American Trade Unions', in Zollschan, G. K. and Hirsch, W. (eds.) *Explorations in Social Change*, London: Routledge and Kegan Paul, pp. 749–77

Marsh, A. (1965) *Industrial Relations in Engineering*, Oxford: Pergamon

Martin, R. (1968) 'Union Democracy: An Explanatory Framework', *Sociology* 2, pp. 205–20

(1977) *The Sociology of Power*, London: Routledge and Kegan Paul

Michels, M. (1958) *Political Parties*, New York: Free Press

Moran, M. (1974) *The Union of Post Office Workers*, London: Macmillan

Mouzelis, M. P. (1975) *Organization and Bureaucracy*, London: Routledge and Kegan Paul

National Board for Prices and Incomes (1967) *Productivity Agreements*, Report No. 36, London: HMSO

Nichols, T. and Armstrong, P. (1976) *Workers Divided*, London: Fontana

Nichols, T. and Beynon, H. (1977) *Living with Capitalism*, London: Routledge and Kegan Paul

Perrow, C. (1973) 'The neo-Weberian Model: Decision-making, Conflict, Technology', in Salaman G. and Thompson K. (eds.) *People and Organisations*, London: Longman

Pettigrew, A. (1973) *The Politics of Organizational Decision-Making*, London: Tavistock

Phelps-Brown, E. H. (1959) *The Growth of British Industrial Relations*, London: Macmillan

Political and Economic Planning (1948) *British Trade Unionism*, London: PEP

Poole, M. (1975) 'A Power Analysis of Workplace Labour Relations', *Industrial Relations Journal* 7, pp. 31–43

Pribecevik, B. (1957) *The Shop Steward Movement and Workers' Control*, Oxford: Blackwell

Ramaswamy, E. (1977) 'The Participatory Dimension of Trade Union Democracy: A Comparative Sociological View', *Sociology* 11, pp. 465–80

Reder, M. W. (1968) 'Job Scarcity and the Nature of Union Power' in McCormick, B. J. and Smith, E. O. (eds.), *The Labour Market*, Harmondsworth: Penguin, pp. 120–42

Richter, I. (1973) *Political Purpose in Trade Unions*, London: George Allen and Unwin

Bibliography

Roberts, B. C. (1956) *Trade Union Government and Administration in Great Britain*, London: Bell

Sayles, L. R. and Strauss, G. (1967) *The Local Union*, New York: Harcourt, Brace and World

Scanlon, H. (1967) 'The Role of Militancy: Interview with Hugh Scanlon' *New Left Review* 46, pp. 3–15

Seidman, J., London, J., Karsh, B., and Tagliocozzo, D. (1958) *The Worker Views His Union*, Chicago: Chicago University Press

Silverman, D. (1968) 'Formal Organizations or Industrial Sociology: Towards a Social Action Analysis of Organizations', *Sociology* 2, pp. 221–38

(1970) *The Theory of Organizations*, London: Heinemann

Smith, C. G. and Ari, O. N. (1963) 'Organizational Control Structure and Member Consensus', *American Journal of Sociology* 69, pp. 623–38

Strauss, A., Murray, D. J. and Potter, D. C. (1971) 'The Hospital and its Negotiated Order' in Castles, F. G., Murray, D. J. and Potter, D. C. (eds.) *Decisions, Organizations and Society*, Harmondsworth: Penguin, pp. 103–23

Tagliacozzo, D. L. (1956) 'Trade Union Government, its Nature and its Problems: A Bibliographical Review 1945–55', *American Journal of Sociology* 61, pp. 554–81

Tannenbaum, A. S. (ed.) (1968) *Control in Organizations*, London: McGraw Hill

(1968) 'Mechanisms of Control in Local Trade Unions' in A. S. Tannenbaum (ed.) *Control in Organizations*, London: McGraw Hill

Tannenbaum, A. S. and Khan, R. (1958) *Participation in Union Locals*, Evanston, Illinois: Row Peterson

Tannenbaum, A. S., Kavcic, B., Rosner, M., Vianello, M. and Wieser, G. (1974) *Hierarchy in Organizations*, London: Jossey-Bass

Tatlow, A. (1953) 'The Underlying Issues of the 1949–50 Engineering Wage Claim', *Manchester School of Economics and Social Sciences* 21 pp. 258–70

Taylor, R. (1980) *The Fifth Estate*, London: Pan

Trades Union Congress (1960) *Report of the General Council to the 92nd Trades Union Congress*, London: TUC

Turner, H. A. (1950) 'The Crossley Strike', *Manchester School of Economic and Social Sciences* 18, pp. 179–216

(1962) *Trade Union Growth, Structure and Policy*, London: George Allen and Unwin

Van de Vall, N. (1970) *Labour Organizations*, Cambridge: Cambridge University Press

Walton, R. E. and McKersie, R. B. (1965) *A Behavioural Theory of Labour Negotiations*, New York: McGraw Hill

Bibliography

Warner, M. (1972) 'Trade Unions and Organizational Theory: A Preliminary Analysis of Union Environment, Structure and Performance', *Journal of Industrial Relations* 14, pp. 47–62

Webb, S. and B. (1920) *Industrial Democracy*, London: Longman
(1956) *History of Trade Unionism*, London: Longman

Index